BETTER BIDDING WITH BERGEN

Volume II – Competitive Bidding, Fit Bids & More

by Marty Bergen

Published by Max Hardy
P.O. Box 28219, Las Vegas, NV 89126-2219

First Printing, October 1986
Second Printing, November, 1988
Third Printing, December 1990

TABLE OF CONTENTS

INTRODUCTION

BIDDING AFTER OPPONENTS OPEN
After Opponents' 1NT Opening – 1, Landy – 1, Ripstra – 3, Becker – 4, Astro – 4, Brozel – 5, Questions After Opponents' 1NT Opening – 6, Jump Overcalls – 8, Strong Jump Overcall – 9, Intermediate Jump Overcall – 9, Weak Jump Overcall – 10, We Overcall – 12, Other Overcall Situations – 15, Fast Arrival – 16, Michaels Cuebid – 19, Questions on Michaels – 23, Unusual Notrump – 23, Questions on Unusual Notrump – 28, Responding to Unusual Notrump – 29.

DOUBLES – BUT NOT FOR PENALTY
The Negative Double – 31, Questions on Negative Doubles – 33, Responsive Doubles – 39, Support Doubles – 43, Questions on Support Doubles – 47, Doubles – After We Open the Bidding – 50.

COMPETING AFTER WE OPEN
We Bid and Raise (And RHO Interferes) – 52, Negative Free Bids – 54, Opener's Responses to an NFB – 58, Bidding Over the Opponents' Takeout Double – 62, Unusual vs. Unusual, Unusual vs. Michaels – 70, Questions on Unusual vs. Unusual, Unusual vs. Michaels – 75, Lebensohl – 76, Questions on Lebensohl – 78 – Lebensohl After Weak Two-Bids – 80, Questions on Lebensohl After Weak Two-Bids – 81.

FIT BIDS
Fit Showing Bids – 83, Lead-Directing Raises – 85, More Lead-Directing Raises – 87, After a Fit is Found – 89, "Fits," Suits or Splinters – 98, Defining Some Ambiguous Auctions – 100 –, Fit Bids Involving Minor Suits – 103, Cuebids – Mostly Fit Showing – 105, Cuebids Once Again – 108, More Cuebids – 110.

THE MANY FACES OF 2NT
The Good-Bad 2NT – 112, After an Invitational 2NT – 124, Quiz on 2NT Invitational When the Opponents Have Bid – 126, Quiz on Non-Competitive Auctions After 2NT Invitational – 128, The Scrambling 2NT – 130, Responding to a Scrambling 2NT – 133, The Jacoby 2NT Revisited – 137.

INTRODUCTION

When asked by Marty Bergen last year to write the Introduction for his first book, I was happy to oblige; he is a likeable young man. I was a bit curious as to why I had been chosen. After all, I'm not exactly a proponent of Marty's ideas on bidding. However, it was explained to me that I really was qualified based on my years of experience in commenting on Marty's "bids" in *The Bridge World*.

Marty's book on uncontested auctions has been well received by players at all levels, which is no small feat. Some praise the clarity of the writing, others the innovative ideas, while many rave about what the book has done for their own partnerships. While I understand all of the above, my personal favorite was the page that immediately follows the Table of Contents.

Now we have Marty's second book which deals mostly with competitive bidding, an area in which he has had **LOTS** of experience. This book is a nice combination of Standard American as well as standard Bergen, so while I cannot give it a rating of "G," it's not the "XX" that I had expected.

I also found it quite clever of Marty to so thoroughly enlighten his readers (potential opponents) on the topic of non-penalty doubles. However, he didn't fool me. Although I'll certainly make use of many of the conventional doubles that Marty wrote about, I also won't forget the one double that M.B. would never write about, the good old P.D.O.B. (Penalty Double of Bergen).

EDGAR KAPLAN
July 1986

After Opponent's
1 NT Opening

Bridge theorists have long appreciated the preemptive effect of the 1 NT opening bid. The opponents must begin describing their hands at the two-level, and they must do so with care. With 1 NT showing a good balanced hand, opener's partner is in a strong position to judge whether penalties can be inflicted on the opponents. With opener's strength a known quantity, not much more than a good trump holding is required.

In order to capitalize on the idea of making the bidding difficult for the opponents, some players use an opening bid of 1 NT with a weaker hand than the traditional 16–18 or the modern 15–17. This "weak notrump" of 13–15, 12–14, or even 10–12 high card points relies on the sound premise that hands of these modest ranges will occur significantly more frequently than the strong notrumps.

Theorists have been kept busy dealing with the problem of bidding after an opponent's 1 NT opening. Most agree that against the commonly played strong notrump (15–17 or 16–18), the goals should be to get into the auction, to try to go plus and to disturb the security of the opponents' 1 NT contract, which is a murderous contract to defend. Getting to a good game is not usually worth worrying about, since opener has a good enough hand to make an opposing game unlikely.

The theorists also tend to agree that bidding methods should be more concerned with two-suited hands. The reasons for this are:
(1) Two-suited hands occur more frequently.
(2) There is added flexibility because of two choices instead of one.
(3) Two-suited hands tend to play well in one of the suits yet don't contribute much to the defense. One-suited hands with a good suit can often be lethal defending 1 NT.

Still, we would like to have bids available to show one-suited major hands. In addition to the higher scoring aspect, it is much more difficult for the opponents to compete over two of a major than over 2♣ or 2♢. Therefore, most of the conventions preserve the 2♡ and 2♠ overcall of 1 NT as natural bids.

In this study of conventional ways to overcall 1 NT, we will limit ourselves to an examination of the most popular ones.

We begin with Landy, which is No. 1 in both number of followers and simplicity. 2♢, 2♡, and 2♠ all show one-suited hands usually with six or more cards in the suit. (It is much too easy to acquire permanent scars if you frequently overcall 1 NT with indifferent five-card suits.) Partner will usually pass the overcall, but can raise with a good fit, or can introduce a new suit if appropriate.

The conventional bid to show two suits is 2♣. This is used to indicate the most useful two-suited hand, namely the major two-suiter. The 2♣ bidder would like to have 5–5 in the majors with the strength concentrated in the two suits, such as

♠ K Q 10 9 5   ♡ A J 10 6 4   ◇ 8   ♣ 7 5,

but we live in an imperfect world. Nine cards are sometimes held, but one must have good suits and a reasonable number of high cards.

♠ A K J 5   ♡ Q J 10 6 4   ◇ 9 4 3   ♣ 8

would be okay, although once in a while you will catch partner with a revolting hand.

Even 4–4 is possible, although exceptional.

♠ K Q J 5   ♡ A K J 6   ◇ 8   ♣ 10 6 5 4

looks Landy-ish, but it must be about this obvious. Vulnerability is clearly relevant, since it is so easy for the opponents to double you. In the balancing seat, one can take liberties on shapely hands since partner is marked with cards. I would happily bid 2♣ in the balancing seat with

♠ Q 8 7 4 3   ♡ Q 6 5 4 3   ◇ 8   ♣ 9 4,

but partner must be aware that unless the fit is superb, he should restrain himself from leaping to the stratosphere.

A further word about balancing that will hold true with all our conventions: when passout seat has a very weak distributional hand, it is safe for him to bid as long as he can show his shape. But the partnership must have the realistic understanding that a partscore is the limit of their sights. The auction 1 NT – Pass – Pass – ? signifies opener's side has "about" half the deck (although as many as 25 points are possible), so whatever you don't hold, your partner must.

Another reasonable idea which has gained converts is that since a penalty double by a passed hand is impossible, double by a passed hand asks for majors and 2♣ is then freed to show *clubs!*

The responses to Landy:
Pass – a lot of clubs and no interest in the majors.
2◇ – a lot of diamonds and no interest in the majors.
2♡, 2♠ – signoffs with at least three cards in the suit – four if you are lucky.
2 NT – A forcing inquiry to elicit more information from the overcaller. In general the longer major will be bid but occasionally a minor suit fragment (3 or more cards) is shown.
3♣, 3◇ – invites game with a magnificent suit.
3♡, 3♠ – invitational to game, based on lots of trumps.
4♡, 4♠ – Not likely, but with

♠ A 10 7 5 4   ♡ 6   ◇ A 7 4 3   ♣ 10 5 3,

bid 4♠ in response to Landy with confidence.

Try these hands in response to 2♣:

2

1.   ♠ A 4   ♡ K 5 4   ◇ 8 5 4 3   ♣ 10 6 4 2

Bid 2♡. You were asked to take a choice.

2.   ♠ A 6   ♡ 6 5   ◇ 7 4 3   ♣ Q J 10 7 4 3

Pass. Partner will be surprised to be left in 2♣, but it should all be for the best.

3.   ♠ K J 10 5   ♡ 9 8 4   ◇ A 9 8 4 2   ♣ 6

Bid 3♠. This invites partner to go to game, but gives him room in case he was being frisky.

4.   ♠ Q J 5   ♡ K 10   ◇ A 6 5 4   ♣ K 10 7 4

Bid 2 NT. This is an amazingly good hand for this auction. We will hope to hear a 3♠ bid by partner, showing five spades, so we can raise to game. If partner bids something else, we will then bid 3♠ showing a very good hand with only three spades, inviting game. Since we rarely look for game after the opponent's strong notrump, with only three of partner's major the sequence of 2 NT followed by three of a major must be quite a nice hand.

The Landy bidder will almost always pass if his partner bids two of a major, but can bid on with a very big distributional hand, usually 6–5 or better. He shouldn't get carried away though, since a 2♡ response to 2♣ can be made with

♠ 8 7   ♡ 5 4 3   ◇ 8 7 4 3   ♣ 10 9 5 2.

If opponents are using weak notrumps when you Landy, everything is the same, except the partnership is more likely to desire to play in game. The requirements for the Landy bid are basically unchanged.

How do we defend against Landy if the opponents use it against us? A double of 2♣ shows a fair to good responding hand, with some interest in defending. This sets up a forcing auction for the partnership, either of whom will double the opponents with a useful trump holding. If we can't double them, we will go on and do our own thing. 2◇ and 3♣ are natural and competitive after 1 NT–2♣–?, and opener will usually pass. 2 NT and 3 NT are natural, although 2 NT is more competitive than invitational. 2♡ and 2♠ are cuebids, with 2♡ showing a moderate minor suit hand (other two suits) while 2♠ is a game-going cuebid guaranteeing a good offensive hand with length in both minors. We can see that most good hands begin with a double.

Next we will investigate other popular conventions in defense to an opening bid of 1 NT.

The first and least complicated of these is Ripstra, which is almost identical to Landy, our last subject. Instead of using 2♣ to show only majors as in Landy, we bid our longer minor in Ripstra to ask for a major suit preference. Therefore, bid 2♣ with

♠ K Q 8 4   ♡ A J 7 5 3   ◇ 8   ♣ A 10 4,

but bid 2◇ with

♠ A Q 9 7 4   ♡ K J 10 5 4   ◇ 10 4 2   ♣ —.

The advantage of this is that we can indicate a possible alternative contract if partner can't stand the majors. We are also giving a more complete description of our hand to partner. The only price we pay for this is giving up the opportunity to bid a natural 2 ♦.

Another convention which grew out of Landy uses a 2 ♣ bid to show minors, while 2 ♦ is the major suit takeout. This convention is sometimes referred to as "modified Landy"; others call it "Becker" although it is not clear which Becker, if any, originated it. It is a convenient way to show a minor two-suiter at the two-level. A sample hand for 2 ♣ would be

♠ 10 4   ♡ 8   ♦ K Q 7 5 3   ♣ A Q J 5 4.

Of course, for each conventional bid that you adopt, you lose a natural bid. Playing either Becker or Ripstra, we can no longer bid 2 ♦ over 1 NT with

♠ 8   ♡ K 6 5   ♦ K Q J 10 3 2   ♣ K 5 2,

which is unfortunate; and with Landy we cannot bid 2 ♣ with

♠ A Q J   ♡ 8 6 3   ♦ 9   ♣ K Q J 10 9 5,

showing length and strength in clubs. With

♠ K 7 5   ♡ 8   ♦ A K J 10 6 5   ♣ J 8 4,

bid 2 ♦ if using Landy, but this bid would be conventional if using either Becker or Ripstra, so you would have to bid 3 ♦ or pass.

All our notrump defense conventions so far utilize the major suit overcalls as natural bids. We will see that in a few of the more complicated conventions this cannot be assumed.

Another convention with a significant number of followers is Astro. Like most of our conventions so far, Astro emphasizes the major suits. However, it differs from the aforementioned conventions in that your two suits may consist of one major and one minor. 2 ♣ shows hearts and a lower suit while 2 ♦ shows a two-suiter, one suit being spades and the other being any one of the remaining three. 2 ♡ and 2 ♠ are retained as natural bids.

How does partner respond to Astro? Responder bids the major shown by overcaller when holding three or more, but sometimes will bid a long suit of his own. If you don't have something good to do, you relay with the cheapest suit to ask the overcaller to identify the second suit. With

♠ 9   ♡ K J 5 4   ♦ K 10 7 4   ♣ J 8 7 3

after 1 NT – 2 ♦ – Pass, bid 2 ♡ prepared for anything. Your partner will pass with a heart suit, rebid a very good spade suit, or bid three of his minor if that's his second suit.

Do notice, though, that you should be well-prepared to use the "relay" bid. You must be prepared for anything since partner's second suit is temporarily unknown. This is the disadvantage of Astro. The advantage is that you can use Astro much more often than the others, as you have a way to show a major-minor two-suiter, a common hand type.

A 2 NT response to the Astro bidder asks the overcaller to identify his second suit at the three-level, based on a very attractive hand for the responder. 2 NT is also used by the overcaller to show a minor two-suiter, which should be based on at least 5–5 since the responder is forced to the three-level.

Try these potential overcalling hands over 1 NT, assuming you are using Astro. Assume that neither side is vulnerable and RHO opens 1 NT (15–17).

1.   ♠ A K 7 4 3   ♡ J 10 6 4 3   ◊ K 5   ♣ 8

Bid 2 ◊. This shows spades and a lower suit.

2.   ♠ K 7   ♡ K Q J 10 4   ◊ A 5   ♣ J 7 4 3

Bid 2 ♡. It must be better to treat this as a one-suiter in the strong major, rather than a two-suiter with the mangy clubs.

3.   ♠ 9   ♡ 10 6   ◊ A J 10 9 7 4 2   ♣ A J 3

Bid 3 ◊. 2 ◊ would promise spades.

4.   ♠ A 6   ♡ 9 2   ◊ K Q J 10 6   ♣ A Q 10 4

Double. You have no reasonable call at the two-level, and it would not be surprising to collect a juicy penalty with this hand.

5.   ♠ Q 6   ♡ K J 7 4   ◊ Q 5   ♣ A J 7 5 3

Pass. You won't be able to play in 2 ♣ and this hand does not have enough playing strength to enter the auction in the direct seat.

The last of the popular conventions to consider is Brozel. This convention makes the assumption that good penalty doubles against the opponents' strong notrumps occur rarely, and someone usually runs out anyway. Some players do not agree with this view so Brozel will appeal only to certain players. A powerful argument for Brozel is that you can bid most one and two-suited hands while remaining at the two-level.

All one-suited hands (in Brozel) commence with a conventional double of 1 NT. Partner should bid 2 ♣ to allow the doubler to identify his suit. The only justification for not bidding 2 ♣ is a very long suit in the responding hand, or a very strong *balanced* hand that will try to defeat 1 NT.

Since all one-suited hands are shown by doubling 1 NT, all two-level overcalls promise two-suiters. Here is the schedule:

> 2 ♣ clubs and hearts
> 2 ◊ diamonds and hearts
> 2 ♡ hearts and spades
> 2 ♠ spades and a minor
>   (partner can discover which
>   minor by responding 2 NT)

The key to remembering Brozel is that the minor suit overcalls show the suit bid plus hearts.

Which of these conventions is the best way to handle opponent's *2 NT openings?* You will not want to bid very often in any case, but two-suiters worth a bid will occur on occasion. You should play the same as you do against

1 NT, but make sure that you and partner understand what you're doing. What would you bid over 1 NT with this hand:

♠ K J 10 8 7 4   ♡ –   ◇ A K J 6 4 3   ♣ 9?

Most conventions have no completely forcing bid to cater to this kind of freak, but some experts play that a 2 NT overcall shows a monstrous two-suiter like the one above. Partner usually responds 3♣ to make it easy for the 2 NT bidder to clarify which suits are held.

While on the subject of monstrous two-suiters, what would you think partner meant if he overcalled 1 NT with 3 NT or 4 NT? Since these could hardly be natural, let's say that since 3 NT forces to the 4-level and 4 NT to the 5-level, that 3 NT shows majors and 4 NT minors, about 6–6 or so. Don't be surprised if this auction doesn't come up often.

We have now described a number of conventions for you to use if you want, or to understand if your opponents use them against you. But how do you defend when the opposition trots them out?

Recommended defense for all of these is similar to the one described regarding Landy.

Double – Good hand, interested in defending.

Cheapest cue – Moderate takeout for the other suits.

Second cue (if available) – Good hand, takeout for other suits.

Non-jump bid – Competitive, non-forcing and non-invitational.

Jump bid – Natural, invitational.

2 NT – Competitive.

Keep in mind that when we say "cuebid" we mean a bid in a suit the opponents have *shown*, regardless of what they have *bid*. For example, after 1 NT – 2♣ (Astro), 3♣ is natural, 2♡ would be the cuebid.

Since the Brozel double is an artificial action which consumes no bidding room, it is suggested that you ignore it and have your responses mean exactly what they would without the double. Therefore, 1 NT – Dbl – 2♣ would be Stayman just like 1 NT – Pass – 2♣. 1 NT – Dbl – 2♡ would mean the same as 1 NT – Pass – 2♡, etc. Of course, redouble would show a good hand and a desire to penalize the opponents if they run, just as it would over a real business double.

This concludes our study of conventional defenses to 1 NT openers. You and your partner should select one that you both understand and which seems to handle your relevant problems.

Since each has good and bad points, sophistication is not the key. If you can find an opportunity to enter the auction and go plus in a reasonable trump suit, you're doing just fine.

Questions After Opponents' 1 NT Opening

Question: **I held**

♠ K J 10 8 7 4   ♡ 8   ◇ 6 5 3   ♣ 9 4 2

after my partner's 1 NT opening and was all set to transfer to a cozy 2♠ contract when my opponent interfered with Landy. What should I have done?

Answer: It would have been nice if two spades were natural here, unfortunately it is not. All you can do is pass 2♣ and wait to balance in spades, presumably over 2♡. That should be natural, just like

1♣	Pass	1♡	Pass
1♠	2♣		

Question: **When the opponents use Landy, what should jump cuebids of 3♡ and 3♠ mean?**

Answer: Splinter bids, showing shortness in the suit bid with game-forcing values. After 1 NT–(Opp.)2♣, bid 3♡ with

♠ A 9 4   ♡ 8   ◊ K Q J 6   ♣ J 8 7 4 3.

Question: **I held**

♠ K Q J 10 7 4 3   ♡ 8   ◊ A K J 6   ♣ 9

and intended to bid Gerber after my partner opened 1 NT. However my opponent overcalled with an Astro 2♣. Would 4♣ still be ace-asking, or should I have bid 4 NT?

Answer: As long as a jump to 4♣ is available, you need not change your methods, so 4♣ would be Gerber and 4 NT quantitative. However, if the opponent's overcall does not allow a jump to 4♣ (being 3♣ or higher), then 4♣ would no longer be Gerber, and further partnership discussion would be required. Perhaps 4 NT quantitative with a jump to 5♣ for Gerber is as good as anything.

Question: **I ran up against opponents who used an overcall of 2♣ over our 1 NT as a one-suiter, with the suit unspecified. What would you suggest as a defense?**

Answer: We play that Dbl is Stayman, and all other bids mean exactly the same as if the opponent had passed, so 2◊ **is a transfer to hearts, etc.**

We also play that after any artificial double of 1 NT, we ignore it and play "front of card," as if the opponent had passed.

Question: **What should a double of 2 NT mean?**

Answer: It shouldn't be for penalties as far as I'm concerned, but then again, I even prefer artificial Dbls over 1 NT. Assuming that overcalls of 2 NT are natural, then Dbl should show a two-suiter. If direct overcalls would promise two suits (my preference), then Dbl should be Brozelish, promising a one-suiter.

Question: **If we use Lebensohl after the opponents one-suited overcalls, should we also employ that vs. Landy and other two-suited bids?**

Answer: Sure, why not. But bidding any *known* suit should be a cue bid. So if 2♣ promises clubs and a higher suit, 3♣ should be a cue bid (like Stayman), not a forcing club hand.

Jump Overcalls

The question of how to treat a jump overcall like opp: 1♦, you; 2♡ has been one without universal agreement for a long time. For many years the jump overcall was used to show a very *strong* hand, something like

♠ K Q 5 ♡ A K Q 9 6 4 ♦ 6 3 ♣ K 7.

This worked well when it occurred, but admittedly the chances of picking up a hand like the one above after an opponent has opened are quite small.

This hand could still be handled without the jump overcall by making a takeout double and bidding strongly thereafter. Therefore, many tournament players decided that the strong treatment for jump overcalls was impractical. Some of them decided to use the jump overcall to show an *intermediate* type of hand—one with an opening bid and a good six-card suit, for example

♠ A 7 ♡ K Q J 8 6 4 ♦ 8 5 ♣ K 7 4.

Others went whole hog and took up *weak* jump overcalls to designate a hand which resembles a weak two bid, something like

♠ 8 4 ♡ Q J 10 9 7 3 ♦ 5 ♣ K 10 6 5.

Before taking a close look at each of these, it is important to clarify two points. In the balancing or pass-out seat, the jump overcall was and is invariably played as intermediate. This is necessary to distinguish between a hand like

♠ A 6 3 ♡ Q J 9 8 4 ♦ 7 ♣ 10 7 5 4

where you bid merely to keep the auction alive from a pretty good hand like

♠ A 6 3 ♡ A K 10 9 7 4 ♦ 7 ♣ 10 7 3.

If you have a normal weak jump overcall in the balancing seat, simply bid your suit at the minimum level, trusting partner to be aware that you may just be "balancing."

It is also necessary to avoid confusing jump overcalls which are single jumps like the aforementioned opp: 1♦, you: 2♡, from the pure preemptive double jumps like opp: 1♦, you: 3♡. These, of course, are universally played as preemptive and resemble opening three bids, for instance

♠ 8 ♡ K Q J 10 6 4 3 ♦ 9 3 ♣ Q 7 4.

We are now ready to examine the three types of jump overcalls as played today. After doing so, we will conclude with a comparison of all three to see the differences and similarities.

8

Strong Jump Overcall

This shows a very good hand with a fine six- or seven-card suit. The number of high card points is not nearly as important as the number of playing tricks, which should be close to eight. All of these would be suitable for a strong jump overcall after an opponent opened 1 ◊.

♠ A Q J 10 6 5	♡ A 7	◊ K 8	♣ A 6 4
♠ 9 4	♡ A 5	◊ K 7 2	♣ A K Q J 7 4
♠ K 7	♡ A K J 10 9 4 3	◊ 9	♣ A 5 4

Partner is not forced to respond, but obviously does not need much to keep the auction open. Because of the length and strength shown by the strong jump overcaller's suit, responder will usually raise his partner with a few scattered values, but bids in notrump and responder's own suit are also possible. New suits would be considered forcing. Of course, if the strong jump overcall is in a minor, partner generally will prefer notrump to a raise.

Very few people still use strong jump overcalls today.

Intermediate Jump Overcall

This is more commonly seen on the West coast; in the East virtually everyone has gone to weak jump overcalls. The intermediate jump overcall is a hand worth an opening bid with a strong six-card suit. The high card point count will usually be about 12-14, but more importantly, the hand should have about 6½ playing tricks. Here are some examples of intermediate jump overcalls after an opponent opens 1 ♡:

♠ K Q J 10 7 4	♡ A 7	◊ Q 10 4	♣ 5 3
♠ 10 6	♡ 9 3	◊ A K Q J 8 4	♣ A 5 3
♠ Q 9 4	♡ 8	◊ A 7 4	♣ A K J 10 9 4

Notice that the three-level bids tend to be a little stronger than the two-level bids.

If you play intermediate jump overcalls, you have to decide what to do with hands that would normally be considered weak jump overcalls, such as

♠ A Q J 10 9 4   ♡ 8   ◊ 9 6 3   ♣ 10 7 5.

Presumably you will want to bid spades, so you'll say 1 ♠. Because the modern tendency is to treat overcalls like opening bids, you will have to hope that bidding with a hand this weak will not mislead partner.

The responses to intermediate jump overcalls are similar to those after strong jump overcalls, keeping in mind that intermediate jump overcalls are about an ace lighter. Therefore, responder needs about an ace more. 2 NT and the single raise are still invitational, and new suits are also forcing, since partner will not need to be rescued from his suit.

Try these hands after 1 ◊ –2 ♡ –Pass, playing intermediate jump overcalls.

1)   ♠ K 4 3 2   ♡ 8 6   ◊ A Q 7   ♣ Q J 5 4

Bid 3 NT. This should have a good play, and if partner prefers 4♡, that's OK also.

2)   ♠ Q 5 4 3   ♡ 8   ◊ K J 7 3   ♣ K J 4 3

Pass. With another heart, 2 NT would be reasonable.

3)   ♠ 9 4   ♡ A 7 5   ◊ 10 6 4 2   ♣ A 7 4 3

Bid 3♡. Game is still possible if partner has a maximum.

Weak Jump Overcall

The modern tendency is to preempt actively to induce the opponents into making errors by being forced to guess at higher levels. The weak jump overcall is always less than an opening bid, with about 6–10 high card points and a good six-card suit. These of course, are the approximate requirements for a weak two bid so it's easy to see why these bids are often thought of in the same light. Here are some examples of weak jump overcalls after the opponents open 1◊ :

♠ K Q J 10 7 4   ♡ 6 5 4   ◊ 7 3 2   ♣ 8
♠ 8 4 2   ♡ Q J 10 8 6 3   ◊ A 5 4   ♣ 6
♠ 5   ♡ K 7 4   ◊ 9 4   ♣ Q J 10 7 6 4 2

Notice that in my example of a weak jump overcall in clubs, I included a seventh club. Since weak jump overcalls are preemptive bids where you do not anticipate making your contract, level and vulunerability become more crucial than with strong jump overcalls and intermediate jump overcalls. It is comforting to have a seven-card suit when going to the three-level and/or when vulnerable. Since a seven-card suit occurs much less often, you will sometimes make the weak jump overcall with a six-card suit.

Some advocates of weak jump overcalls even go so far as to play intermediate jump overcalls when the vulnerability is unfavorable or they must bid at the three level. This is obviously a reasonable idea, although I prefer to play that the jump overcall is always weak but assure partner that I will be more careful at these moments.

Weak jump overcalls also offer the opportunity to "operate" a little at matchpoints when partner passes and we are non-vulnerable. Just as I would open 2♠ in third seat non-vulnerable with

♠ K Q J 10 6   ♡ 6 4 3   ◊ 10 7 5 2   ♣ 8,

I would bid 2♠ after Pass–Pass–1♣ even with only five spades.

The responses to weak jump overcalls resemble those after weak twos, rather than those after intermediate jump overcalls or strong jump overcalls. Raises are non-invitational, merely an attempt to continue the preempt. Many use the 2 NT bid just the same as they do over an opening weak two. Others play 2 NT as invitational, showing about an opening 1 NT bid. New suits are not treated as forcing, which may differ from what you play over weak twos. Strength showing cuebids can also be made here, as they can with any jump overcall.

Try responding with these hands after partner has made a weak jump overcall in this auction 1♡-2♠-Pass. (Neither side is vulnerable.)

1) ♠ K 10 6   ♡ 9 4 3   ◇ A 7 5   ♣ 8 6 4 3

Bid 3♠. Don't expect to buy it for 2♠. Where are all the good cards? Opener is virtually a lock to reopen and possibly get to game, so throw in your 2¢ now. This is the same action you should take over a weak 2♠ opening by partner.

2) ♠ —   ♡ A 10 7 4   ◇ Q J 9 8 6 3   ♣ Q 5 2

Pass. Parner's diamond support is probably better than your spade support. However, 3◇ has little to recommend it. "No double, no trouble," is appropriate here, so don't scream for help until you are in real danger.

3) ♠ Q 8 7 2   ♡ A   ◇ 6 4 3   ♣ A 10 6 5 4

Bid 4♠. There is no way to know if you can make it, but it could be cold even opposite a minimum if partner has the right hand. Also, aren't you going to have to bid it eventually when the opponents go to 4♡?

One problem with weak jump overcalls is that there is no longer a direct efficient way to show the intermediate jump overcall type hand which does have a chance for game. All you can do is make a simple overcall, and then rebid it if convenient to show the fair hand with the six-card suit.

An advantage of weak jump overcalls is that the simple overcall now usually shows a fair hand, similar to an opening bid. Therefore, responder is on more familiar ground in responding and doesn't have to worry too much about partner having "just an overcall." With a weak hand but good suit you now either make the weak jump overcall or forget about the hand completely.

	STRONG	INTERMEDIATE	WEAK	WEAK AT THREE-LEVEL AND/OR VUL.
cards in suit	6 or 7	6	6	preferably 7
high card points (based on 6 card suit)	16–18 (fewer with seven-card suit)	12–14	6–10	6–10
suit quality	excellent — usually 3 of top 4 honors	good quality — 2 of top 3 or 3 of top 5 honors	usually 3 of top 6 honors (more flexible if not vul.)	3 of top 5
playing tricks	7½–8½	5½–7	4½–5½	5–6
raise	invitational	invitational	preemptive	preemptive
2NT	invitational	invitational	same as with weak two	same as with weak two
new suit	forcing	forcing	non-forcing	non-forcing

Summary

The jump overcall works nicely as a descriptive bid for partner and a pre-emptive bid against the opponents. Since the weak hands have the greatest frequency, the majority of players have adopted them. They work nicely on the same principle as weak two bids. Intermediate jump overcalls also have their advocates as well as their advantages. Most players agree that the jump overcall, like the cuebid, is too valuable a bid to waste on a hand so strong that it will rarely occur.

We Overcall

Assume partner has overcalled an opening 1♣ bid with 1♡ with neither side vulnerable. Our overcalls have a wide range – they can be *occasionally light* or *real rocks*. Here are samples:

♠ 8 6	♡ A Q J 10	◇ K 7 4	♣ 10 8 7 5
♠ 9	♡ A Q 7 4 2	◇ K 5	♣ A K J 7 4
♠ A J 7 4	♡ A K 9 5 3	◇ 8	♣ 10 7 2
♠ 9 4	♡ K J 8 7 5	◇ A 10 6 3	♣ 5 2
♠ A 6 4	♡ A Q 9 7 4 3	◇ 8	♣ A 10 6
♠ K 6	♡ A J 9 8 6 4 3	◇ Q 5	♣ K 4

We will treat a new suit as non-forcing after a one-level overcall. However, that doesn't mean the overcaller will go out of his way to pass. Let's detail the responses after 1♣–1♡–Pass.

1♠, 1 NT, 2◇ –Nonforcing, could be reasonable hands. The suit bids show good suits, particularly the 2◇ bid.

2♣ –Limit heart raise or better. At least three-card support, 10+ points including distribution.

2♡ –Normal single raise, usually three trumps.

2♠, 2 NT, 3◇ –Strongly invitational. The suit bids show good six-card suits.

3♣ –Mixed raise. The jump cuebid after an overcall is played as different things by different people, but I've had good success with this *fit* bid. A mixed raise contains some offense and some defense–hence its name. It is based on a hand with four plus trumps (offense) but is too good for a preemptive jump raise. It has some high cards (defense) but not enough for a limit raise.

Here are some samples of mixed raises.

♠ A 7 4	♡ Q 10 5 2	◇ 8 7 4 3 2	♣ 9
♠ K 6 3	♡ A 7 4 3 2	◇ 9 6	♣ 8 5 4
♠ 9 2	♡ K 8 7 4	◇ K 6	♣ J 10 9 7 5

3 ♡ – The aforementioned weak jump raise, one of my favorite *fit bids*. We guarantee four plus trumps, and that's about all.

♠ 8 7	♡ Q 7 4 2	◇ 9 6 4 3	♣ 7 5 4
♠ 8	♡ J 10 7 5	◇ 9 7 6 5 4	♣ 8 6 3
♠ 8 7 5 4	♡ K J 6 3	◇ 7 5	♣ 9 4 3.

3 ♠, 4 ♣, 4 ◇ – Splinter raise in support of hearts. These don't occur too often, but they are as good as anything. They do suggest a possibility of slam.

3 NT – Natural, also rare. Tends to deny a heart fit, since we didn't begin with a cuebid.

4 ♡ – Preemptive, but may be better than a raise to four opposite an opening bid. Since slam is much less likely after the opponent's opening bid, these hands all qualify:

♠ K 7 4 3 2	♡ A J 9 7 4	◇ 8	♣ 10 6
♠ 10 7 6 5	♡ A Q 9 7 3	◇ 8 7 6	♣ 8
♠ J 10 6 4 3	♡ K 9 7 5 2	◇ 8 7 4	♣ –.

What happens if third hand bids a suit, say 1 ♠? Does that cause much to change?

After 1 ♣ – 1 ♡ – 1 ♠, there are several actions worthy of a look. Any bid not mentioned here is assumed to be unaffected by the 1 ♠ bid.

2 ♠ – This is now a cuebid, providing us with a second choice. We take advantage of that and designate the higher cuebid (2 ♠) as a limit raise or better guaranteeing at least four trumps. Therefore:

2 ♣ – The cheaper cuebid now shows a good raise but with exactly three trumps.

This distinction is often crucial for the partnership to determine, as we've seen in previous situations.

3 ◇ – Only a slight change here. This is now more of a competitive, preemptive bid than an invitational effort. Most experts believe that jumps in competition are best played as preemptive.

Double – With third hand bidding, the possibility of double now exists. Many experts use this double as a third suit double. This shows diamonds (the fourth suit) with tolerance for partner's suit (usually a doubleton). Something like these hands would be reasonable:

| ♠ 9 4 | ♡ K 7 | ◇ K Q 9 7 3 | ♣ 9 7 4 2 |
| ♠ A 7 4 2 | ♡ J 3 | ◇ K J 8 6 4 | ♣ 8 5. |

The other interpretation for a double in this position (it makes no sense as a penalty double, since the opponent is making a forcing bid) is as a Rosenkranz double, showing one of the top three heart honors. Invented by George Rosenkranz of Mexico, this concept was published in the *Bulletin* several years ago. It can be very helpful on defense (especially on lead) since if the double guarantees a heart honor, the pass denies one! We'll be taking a further look at this type of concept when we consider *Rosenkranz Redoubles*.

If instead of a 1 ♣ – 1 ♡ – 1 ♠ beginning, the auction actually starts 1 ♣ – 1 ♡ – 1 NT or 1 ♣ – 1 ♡ – 2 ♣, matters are pretty much the same. There is only one suit to cuebid, so the club limit raise could be any number of trumps more than two. Of course over 2♣ we have to go all the way to the three-level in order to show the limit-plus raise.

Double is now responsive after 1♣ –1♡ –2♣, suggesting length in the unbid suits. After 1♣ –1♡ –1 NT, the double shows some high cards, played as penalty oriented by most, semi-responsive by others. *Semi-responsive* suggests that we are hoping that partner bids something, rather than defending the freely bid 1 NT doubled.

For the following hands, consider what you would do after each of these auctions. Neither side is vulnerable.

1) 1♣ –1♡ –Pass?
2) 1♣ –1♡ –1♠?
3) 1♣ –1♡ –2♣ –?
4) 1♣ –1♡ –1 NT–?

a.	♠ 8 7	♡ Q J 10 6	◇ 10 7 5 4 2	♣ 9 3
b.	♠ 7 4 3	♡ K J	◇ Q J 7 4 2	♣ K 10 4
c.	♠ A 2	♡ K J 9 6	◇ Q 10 8 4	♣ 6 5 4

Answers:

a. 1) 3♡ 2) 3♡ 3) 3♡ 4) 3♡. What could be easier?

b. 1) 1 NT, most flexible. 2) Double, showing diamonds with heart tolerance. 3) 2♡. Your spades aren't adequate for a responsive double and it would be hard to get to hearts if we bid 2◇. 4) Double, showing cards. Preserves all options.

c. 1) 2♣, showing a limit raise. 2) 2♠, showing a limit-plus raise with four-plus trumps. 3) 3♣. No cheaper cuebid. 4) 2♣. Any limit raise.

Our first auction occurs after an opponent's negative double. For example:

$$1♣ –1♡ –Dbl–?$$

A very popular treatment is to use *redouble* to show a high honor in partner's suit, hearts in this instance. This was invented by George Rosenkranz, and is known as a *Rosenkranz Redouble* or as a negative redouble.

If redouble is the proper call holding a high honor (A, K or Q), does that mean that pass denies a high honor? This certainly seems logical, but I play this only after a one-level overcall, which is unlikely to be passed out. Since I believe in redoubling with very weak hands with a high honor, even

♠ 8 6 4 2   ♡ K   ◇ 7 5 4 3   ♣ 9 4 3 2,

I can't risk playing a redoubled contract opposite that, and at the two-level or higher my opponents might choose to defend. By the way, both the negative redouble and the pass denying an honor must be Alerted.

Rosenkranz' original concept was to employ the redouble even with normal single raises, but most experts are not prepared to give up the competitive and preemptive advantages of that bid.

I use the negative redouble with two types of hands. One is the hand with three trumps that is too weak to raise, e.g.,

♠ 9 7 3   ♡ K 6 4   ◇ 8 6 4   ♣ 10 5 4 3.

I also will redouble on hands which don't have enough trumps to raise, like

♠ A 6   ♡ Q 5   ◊ Q 8 6 4 3   ♣ 7 5 4 2

The rest of my raises after 1♣–1♡–Dbl–? are the usual ones I employ after an overcall: 2♣ = limit raise or better, 2♡ = single raise, 3♣ = mixed raise, 3♡ = preemptive raise. The one new bid is 2 NT to show a four-card limit raise, allowing the club cuebid to again promise exactly three trumps. None of these bids either promises or denies a heart honor.

For those who feel that the advantages of the Rosenkranz concept are substantial enough to merit further exploitation, (1♣ – 1♡ – Dbl – ?) play that 2♡ denies a high heart honor, while 2♣ shows a single raise with an honor. 2 NT would now be the only limit raise auction. Since single raises will occur much more often than limit raises, clarifying the honor situation may be worth the price of being forced to the three-level on a three-card limit raise. Imaginative readers may spot other possibilities as well.

Other Overcall Situations

1)   1♠   2♣   Pass   2♡

There is a good case for treating a new suit as forcing by an unpassed hand after a two-level overcall. There is a division among leading players on this topic, but since a two-level overcall tends to resemble an opening bid, treating a new suit as forcing allows the same approach bidding that ensues after an opening bid.

2)   1 NT   2◊   Pass   2♠

Assuming 1 NT to be strong, and 2◊ to be natural, what should 2♠ show? Some would say that it guarantees a diamond fit, looking for bigger and better things. Others would say that it says nothing about diamonds, but shows a good hand with spades and is forcing. For myself, I would treat it primarily as a correction, suggesting that I believe spades will play better than diamonds. Partner can raise with a spade fit, but will usually pass.

3)   3♣   3♡   Pass   3♠

This should clearly be played as forcing. Although it doesn't suggest a heart fit (we would usually cuebid 4♣ with a fit), it is too unlikely that the limit of the hand should be treated as forcing by an unpassed hand following an opponent's preempt.

4)   1♣   Pass   1♡   2♣

The 2♣ bid should be regarded as natural, and many good pairs do have this understanding. Playing five-card majors, an opening 1♣ bid can have a weak enough suit so that an opponent might want to play in clubs.

5)   1♣   Pass   1♡   2♡

This should also be played as a natural overcall. The arguments are similar to those above, and experience has shown this to be a very good tactical bid. I would be happy to overcall 2♡ on

♠ A 7 4   ♡ K Q J 9 6 3   ◇ 9 5 4   ♣ 8.

By the way, it is worth discussing what double by opener means in this case as even most top pairs would be on shaky ground here.

6)   1◇   Pass   1♠   1 NT

I recommend using this as takeout, as overcalling a natural 1 NT against two bidding opponents seems to be risking more than you stand to gain. Good balanced hands after the opponents have bid demand great caution. I might bid 1 NT holding

♠ 8 6   ♡ K 8 7 4 3   ◇ A   ♣ J 7 5 4 2.

I want to compete in one of the unbid suits, but I'm not strong enough to double, nor brave enough for 2 NT.

7)   1♣   1♡   Pass   1♠
                           Pass   2♣

I play the 2♣ bid as a cuebid; perhaps the 1♠ bid really turned the overcaller on. However . . .

8)   1♣   1♡   Pass   1 NT
                           Pass   2♣

I would treat this 2♣ bid as a natural bid, since it is unlikely that the 1 NT response would cause partner to get stars in his eyes, and furthermore it is more likely that one would want to play in clubs when partner promised a reasonable holding in that suit.

However, my preferences for 7) and 8) are certainly not to everyone's taste, so make sure you discuss them with your favorite partners, rather than praying after making the bid that you don't get left in a cuebid!

Fast Arrival

Our discussion of fit bids after overcalls leads us to the important principle of **fast arrival**:

When we agree on a trump suit and are in a forcing auction, bidding the trump suit at the level we are forced to shows the least forward-going type of hand.

Let's look at five sample auctions, on each of which we were forced to compete further.

1)   1♦   1♠   2♠   3♣
                           ?

2♠ was a limit raise or better in diamonds. Regardless of whether responder's raise was limit or forcing, his hand was reasonable enough to warrant further bidding by his side. Therefore, if opener passes 3♣, responder can't pass. A pass by opener is a *forcing pass* – partner is *forced* to take some action.

Opener's pass of 3♣ preserves all options. All of these would be valid reasons for passing 3♣:

a) Holding a hand which doesn't offer an obvious action but is too good to bid 3♦.

b) Offering partner a chance to double 3♣.

c) Encouraging partner to think about game even if he had only a limit raise.

On the other hand, if opener bid 3♦, he would be indicating:

a) A minimum opening bid.

b) No particular desire to defend 3♣ doubled.

c) No game interest opposite a limit raise.

2)   1♠   2♣   Pass   2♠
                           Dbl   ?

Once again, the cuebid of 2♠ showed a limit raise or better. It forced the overcaller's side to compete to at least 3♣.

3♣ is the weakest bid without the double, and it is also weaker than pass after the double. 3♣ shows a very minimum overcall – pass does not.

3)   1♡   Pass   3♣   3♦
                           ?

3♣ = Bergen raise, 4 trumps, 7-10 points including distribution.

Without the 3♦ bid, 3♡ would be the signoff, 3♦ the game try. 3♡ is still the signoff, but pass acts as the game try. Of course, this is a forcing pass, so responder's options include 3♡, 4♡ and double – but not pass.

4)   1♣   1♦   Pass   2♣
                           Dbl   ?

Same old story. 2♦ is the weakest action. The forcing pass implies at least a decent hand.

5)   1♦   1♠   Dbl   3♦
                           Dbl   ?

After the 3♦ mixed raise, which forces us to bid at least 3♠, pass acts as a game try. Notice that we can benefit from the opponents' intervention. If they pass 3♦, our only action below 3♠ is a 3♡ bid, which acts as an all-purpose game try, the only one available. But after they double 3♦, we have

a) Pass = general game try.

b) 3♡ = heart game try.

c) Redouble = Diamond game try or whatever else you wish to us it for.

17

Here are some more auctions governed by fast arrival:

5)   1♡   Pass   4♣   Dbl
                      4♡

After the splinter bid of 4♣ is doubled, opener could pass if he had slam interest, even if it was only a little. The 4♡ bid indicates a complete lack of interest.

7)   1♡   Pass   2NT   Pass
                      3♣   Pass   4♡

2 NT = Jacoby, game forcing heart raise.
3♣ = singleton or void in clubs.

If responder now bids 4♡, that is the weakest action he can take. He presumably has wasted values in clubs, with only a mediocre forcing raise. Opener is allowed to bid again, but only if he has a rock. A typical hand for responder would be

♠ 9 6 4 3   ♡ A J 7 2   ◊ K 5 3   ♣ K Q.

8)   1♡   Pass   2♣   Pass
                      2◊   Pass   2♡   Pass
                      2NT   Pass   4♡

2♣ = Game forcing.

4♡ shows a minimum, 3♡ (or any other action) preserves bidding room and suggests a better hand.

9)   1♡   Pass   2♡   Pass
                      3♣   Pass   3◊

The game try of 3♣ forces our side to at least 3♡. If responder's second bid was 3♡, he would be making the least encouraging bid. We call 3◊ a counter-game try – it's like bidding 3½♡. It's too good for 3♡, not good enough for 4♡. It doesn't really say anything about diamonds.

10)   1NT   Pass   2◊   Pass
                      2♡   Pass   2NT   Pass
                      3◊

2◊ = Jacoby Transfer.

Once again 3◊ is a counter-game try. Presumably this time it shows something in diamonds, since opener also had 3♣ available.

We'll conclude the saga of fast arrival with an important related principle:

When the trump suit has not yet been agreed and a non-jump bid would be forcing, a jump sets trump, promising good ones. But it does not have to be a good hand.

Here are some auctions with corresponding hands. (In each case the hand belongs to the jumper.)

11)   1♣   1♠   ♠ Q 10 6 4 3
                2♡   4♡   ♡ K Q J 4
                                     ◊ 6 3
                                     ♣ 8 4

12)	1♠	2♣	♠ A K Q J 10 6
	3♠		♡ 4 3
2♣ = Game forcing			◊ A 7
			♣ 9 4 2

13)	2♣	2◊	♠ K Q
	3♡		♡ A K Q J 9 4 2
			◊ A K 6
			♣ 8

14)	1♣	2♠	♠ 6
	4♣		♡ 8
			◊ A J 7 4
			♣ K Q J 10 8 7 4

15)	1♣	1♠	♠ A K Q J 5 4
	3♣	4♠	♡ 8 6 4
			◊ 10 7 2
			♣ 9

16)	1NT	2♡	♠ A Q J 8
	2♠	3♣	♡ K 7 5
	4♠		◊ K Q 6
2♡ = Transfer			♣ 9 8 4

♤   ♤

Michaels Cuebid

Some time ago Bridge players realized that using a sequence like

OPP
1◊   2◊

as a game forcing cuebid was very unrealistic since it occurred about as often as Friday the 13th. Therefore, it seemed reasonable to employ the cuebid in a more practical matter, showing a two-suiter, which led to the creation of conventional cuebids such as Michaels, Astro, Colorful, and Top and Bottom.

The most popular and widely used of these is the Michaels cuebid. It is used over both majors and minors, and always shows a two-suited hand.

Any amount of strength is possible with a Michaels cuebid, with vulnerability being quite relevant, but there are guidelines. Let's first look at the major-suited hands, where we are cuebidding the opponents' minor.

The guiding principle here is: It is ok to be very weak or very strong, but try to avoid Michaels on "in-between" hands. With neither side vulnerable,

I would be delighted to use Michaels after an opposing 1♣ opening with any of the following:

1.   ♠ Q J 8 6 4   ♡ K 10 7 4 2   ◇ 8 4   ♣ 8

2.   ♠ Q 10 8 7 4 3   ♡ Q J 5 4 3   ◇ 9   ♣ 8

3.   ♠ A Q J 10 7   ♡ A Q J 10 6   ◇ 8   ♣ A 4

4.   ♠ K Q 9 7 4 2   ♡ A J 10 7 4 3   ◇ —   ♣ 8

With the first two I will have no problem passing when partner responds two of a major. With hands #3 and 4 I won't have any problems either, I will raise "his" major to game. If partner has been forced to take a preference with a hand like

♠ 6 5   ♡ 8   ◇ J 9 7 4 3   ♣ 10 9 6 5 2

this may not work out too well, but this is unlikely (and anyway, I won't have to play it).

The hands that should avoid bidding major suit Michaels are ones like these:

5.   ♠ A Q 8 7 4   ♡ A Q 6 3 2   ◇ 8 5   ♣ 2

6.   ♠ K Q 7 5 3   ♡ A J 6 4 2   ◇ 8   ♣ K 5

The reason is that we won't know what to do after hearing partner's preference. Game could still be on opposite as little as

7.   ♠ J 10 9   ♡ K 7 5   ◇ J 7 4 2   ♣ Q 6 3

but you can hardly bid again when you don't even have a guarantee of a fit. Therefore, when holding "in-between" strength hands, simply overcall one spade intending to bid hearts at your next turn. Even if you are temporarily in the wrong trump suit, someone will usually find a bid when you only have moderate strength and the auction is still at the one-level.

What about major-suit Michaels on 5–4 distribution? I have had very good success with this bid and heartily recommend it, although if you are going to indulge, you should inform your partner so that he doesn't bury you. The four-card suit should be good, and it helps to have the vulnerability in your favorable. Not vul. vs. vulnerable I would bid 2◇ over 1◇ with all of the following:

8.   ♠ Q J 10 6   ♡ Q J 9 6 3   ◇ 8   ♣ 7 4 3

9.   ♠ J 8 6 4 3   ♡ A 10 9 7   ◇ 6 5 4 3   ♣ —

10.   ♠ K J 8 4   ♡ J 10 9 6 5   ◇ 6 4   ♣ 4 2.

When the opening bid has been in a major, the situation is somewhat different. We can no longer afford to bypass Michaels on "middle strength" hands. Otherwise, we may never have the room nor the chance to show both suits. Also, since we will usually be forced to the three-level, the minimum amount of playing strength required is significantly greater. Of course, if you have real shape, you don't need much in high cards. With neither side vul. bid 2♠ over 1♠ with

11.   ♠ 8   ♡ A Q 9 6 4   ◇ K J 10 7 4   ♣ 8 4

or

12.   ♠ 8   ♡ K 9 7 4 3   ◇ A K Q J 5   ♣ Q 5

or even

13.   ♠ —   ♡ K 8 6 4 3 2   ◇ Q 9 7 5 4 3   ♣ 8,

but pass quietly with

14.   ♠ Q 5   ♡ Q 9 7 4 3   ◇ K 8 7 4 3   ♣ K

or

15.   ♠ K 5   ♡ K Q 6 3   ◇ Q 8 7 4 3   ♣ 8 7.

How does partner respond to a Michaels cuebid? Some of the responses are obvious. After 1♠ - 2♠ - Pass - ?,

2 ◇	= Long diamonds, no fit for major
2 ♡, 2 ♠	= Preferences, may have fair hands, but partner is expected to pass lacking a battleship
3 NT	= To play, very rare bid, probably long running minor
4 ♡, 4 ♠	= To play, probably based on great fit

The other responses are not obvious. Some would play

2 NT	= Natural, non-forcing, invitational to game
3 ♣	= Cuebid asking for better or longer major
3 ◇	= Natural, invitational, very good hand
3 ♡, 3 ♠	= Natural invitational

I prefer to use the jumps to three of a major as preemptive, regardless of whether there was action by opener's partner. Some players then play that 3 ♣ is invitational to game in hearts, with 3 ◇ inviting a spade game. The only problem with this is after 1 ◇ - 2 ◇ - Pass - ?, 3 ♣ is needed as natural. Others use 2 NT to start their game invitations with Ogust-type responses:

3 ♣	= Minimum, better or longer hearts
3 ◇	= Minimum, better or longer spades
3 ♡	= Non-minimum, preferring hearts
3 ♠	= Non-minimum, preferring spades
3 NT	= Big hand, surprise, surprise

Try responding with these hands using preemptive jumps and 3♣, 3♢ as game tries. Neither side is vulnerable.

After 1♣ – 2♣ – Pass – ?

(1)	♠ K Q 5 4	3♠	Unless your partner has a moose, the opponents must be cold for something in the minors. If you think that you would buy it for 2♠, you're dreaming.
	♡ Q 8 4		
	♢ 10 7		
	♣ 9 8 6 3		

(2)	♠ Q 10	4♡	Since you have a good play for game opposite as little as K-x-x-x-x, K-x-x-x-x. However if your partner has 5-4 a lot or tends to be a "clown" nonvul, 2 NT would be more prudent, in order to stay out of game when partner was just kidding.
	♡ A Q 10 6		
	♢ 8 7 4 3		
	♣ A 8 5		

(3)	♠ Q 5 4	2♠	is plenty. Most of your minor suit strength is of dubious value for offense.
	♡ J 7		
	♢ K J 5 2		
	♣ K Q 7 4		

If third hand bids, responder need bid only with something of value. If third hand doubles, you must express your preference when holding one, but feel free to pass with equal length.

When partner has cuebid a major suit, you can't be sure which minor he holds. Invariably, the minor you have length in will not match his. A response of 2 NT asks partner to identify his second suit.

After 1♡ – 2♡ – Pass

2♠	=	Nonconstructive
2 NT	=	Asking for minor
3♣, 3♢	=	Natural, signoffs but good suits
3♡	=	Invitational in spades
3♠	=	Preemptive
4♠	=	To play, usually based on fit

Now try these after 1♡ – 2♡ – Pass – ?

♠ Q 4		Bid 2♠. Partner rates to have clubs and spades, so a prudent 2♠ is best.
♡ Q 8 6 4 3		
♢ Q 9 7 4 2		
♣ A		

♠ K 8 7 4 3		Bid 4♠. You will have to bid it eventually over the opponent's 4♡ and there's no time like the present.
♡ 8		
♢ K 6 5		
♣ 10 8 7 4		

♠ 9		Bid 2 NT. Partner will now name his minor, and you are prepared for either one.
♡ K J 7 4		
♢ Q 8 5 4		
♣ K 8 7 6		

♠ J 7
♡ Q 10 8 4
◇ 9
♣ K Q J 10 9 6

Bid 3 ♣. You want to play in clubs despite the fact that partner has spades and diamonds.

Partner should not correct to diamonds over your bid. If he indeed has clubs, you won't mind being raised.

After bidding Michaels, the cuebidder should clam up and leave things to his partner unless he has an exceptional hand. After

1♣	2♣	Pass	2♡
3♣	?		

it is usually correct to pass since partner knows more about your hand than you do about his. After all his 2♡ "bid" could have been made on

♠ 8 3   ♡ Q 7   ◇ K 7 4 3 2   ♣ K J 8 6.

Questions on Michaels

Question: **After 1♠ -2♠ -3♠ -?, is 3 NT natural or does it ask for partner's minor?**

Answer: This requests the minor since that is important to discover, and it is very unlikely that you wish to play in 3 NT.

Question: **If the Michaels bidder doubles at his next turn, what is he signifying?**

Answer: After

1♠	2♠	Pass	2♡
3♣	Dbl		

our hero is showing the unexpected big hand, probably with good defense also.

♠ A K 9 5 4   ♡ A Q 8 6 3   ◇ 8   ♣ A 5

looks right. Partner should be in a good position to know what to do.

Question: **I hate not knowing immediately what minor partner has when he bids Michaels. Is there a sensible way around this?**

Answer: Larry Cohen and I use the cuebid to always show the upper two unbid suits, sort of the opposite of unusual NT. If we have clubs and the other major, we jump to 3♠ as Hi-Lo. This has worked out well, although we do have to give up the WJO in clubs.

Unusual Notrump

The unusual notrump is a convention designed to show two-suited hands, with the emphasis on the minors. It can be likened to the Michaels cuebid, which also shows two suits, although there the emphasis is on the major suits. The unusual notrump usually involves an overcall of 2 NT, but any notrump bid can be "unusual" with the right conditions.

There are two problems with the unusual notrump – one a practical one, the other a theoretical one.

The practical problem is that even experienced players sometimes have trouble identifying "unusual" notrumps as opposed to natural notrump bids. This really does not have to happen in an experienced partnership as long as both players stay on their toes.

The other problem is that the unusual notrump gives away too much distributional information to the opponents, while your chances of outbidding the opponents may be slim. With the minor suits you have to bid "one more" to buy the contract.

For these reasons you should only use the unusual notrump when: the opponents' bidding is moderate, and your side may have a shot at buying the hand; their bidding is so strong that you must suggest a sacrifice; or your hand is so freakish that a moderate fit plus a few useful cards in partner's hand may produce miraculous results.

One further word. One of our most important tasks with the unusual notrump will be to distinguish those notrump bids which show two-suiters from the natural ones showing balanced hands. Although we will have rules to help us, logic and common sense are the keys. Here are our two fundamental guidelines:

(1) An immediate jump to 2 NT is unusual (one exception will be discussed later).

(2) If a notrump bid could reasonably be natural, it is: if it would be unreasonable for a notrump bid to be natural, then it isn't.

It will facilitate our survey of notrump bids if we first examine notrump bids by passed hands. Since we assume that a passed hand is limited to some 12 HCP's most of these notrump bids will be unusual.

YOU	LHO	PARTNER	RHO
Pass	Pass	Pass	1 ♠
1 NT			

or

Pass	Pass	Pass	1 ♡
2 NT			

Clearly, a passed hand could not have the strength to overcall 1 NT or 2 NT, so these hands must be examples of the "unusual" notrump. 1 NT presumably would be 9 or 10 cards in the minors, with 2 NT guaranteeing at least 5 – 5.

YOU	LHO	PARTNER	RHO
Pass	Pass	Pass	1 ◊
1 NT			

or

Pass	Pass	Pass	1 ◊
2 NT			

Since you wouldn't want to get frisky holding length in the opponent's suit, these bids show length in clubs and hearts, the two lower unbid suits. In fact, it is safe to think of all unusual notrump bids as showing the lower two unbid suits, since this also nicely includes minors on auctions where one bids 2 NT over an opponent's 1 ♡ or 1 ♠.

An exception could arise with opponents who play that a minor suit opening could be fewer than 3. Now it is reasonable for 2 NT to show both minors.

YOU	LHO	PARTNER	RHO
Pass	1 ♡	Pass	Pass
1 NT			

or

Pass	Pass	Pass	1 ♡
Pass	1 ♠	Pass	Pass
1NT			

These notrump bids must be regarded as natural balancing bids. For the above auctions, you might hold

♠ K J 8   ♡ K J 6   ◊ Q 6 4 2   ♣ J 10 5.

However, in these auctions:

YOU	LHO	PARTNER	RHO
Pass	1 ♡	Pass	Pass
2 NT			

or

Pass	2 ♡	Pass	Pass
2 NT			

a passed hand could not have enough strength to make a *balancing* 2 NT bid, so both of these 2 NT calls must be *unusual*. You might have something like

♠ K 7   ♡ 9   ◊ Q J 10 9 5   ♣ K J 10 9 6.

We can therefore summarize notrump overcalls by passed hands by saying that all of them are unusual, except for the balancing 1 NT bid.

What about notrump overcalls by an unpassed hand? At the one level they are always natural. 1 ♠ – 1 NT or P – P – 1 ♡ – 1 NT or 1 ♠ – P – P – 1 NT are all natural bids. The first two (the direct ones) show about 15 - 18 HCP. The last, in a balancing auction, could show a balanced hand of about 10 - 15.

In the auction

RHO	YOU
1 ♠	2 NT,

it is unreasonable to expect a hand strong enough to attempt eight tricks in notrump against an opening bid with partner's hand of unknown strength. Therefore, this bid is the "unusual" notrump. You may or may not have an opening bid, but you should always have enough "body" in your two suits so that the roof doesn't fall in when partner holds something like

♠ Q 8 6 4   ♡ K 8 7 5 2   ◊ Q 4   ♣ 9 6.

Though some will disagree, I like to play

LHO	PARTNER	RHO	YOU
1♠	Pass	2♠	2 NT

as unusual. It is unlikely that you will be strong enough to play 2 NT opposite two bidding opponents, so you would double for takeout and bid 2 NT to show the minors.

Also with the opponents in a forcing auction,

LHO	PARTNER	RHO	YOU
1♠	Pass	2◊	2 NT

this must be an "unusual" notrump since the bid cannot be natural. It must show the unbid suits and a very distributional hand like

♠ 8   ♡ K J 10 7 4   ◊ 9   ♣ K J 10 7 4 3.

With a more balanced hand and some defensive strength like

♠ 8   ♡ K Q J 6   ◊ A 5 2   ♣ K Q 9 4 3,

you would say "double" over 2◊.

There is one exception to the rule given earlier that a *jump* to 2 NT is always unusual.

LHO	PARTNER	RHO	YOU
1 suit	Pass	Pass	2 NT

This bid shows a good hand and is a natural bid. The strength is about a 20 count, and it does invite partner to bid 3 NT. This bid is played this way only in the balancing seat.

Let's now turn our attention to some auctions which commence with our opponent opening a weak two-bid:

RHO	YOU	
2♡	2 NT	and

LHO	PARTNER	RHO	YOU
2♡	Pass	Pass	2 NT

These are both natural bids, as you very well might want to play 2 NT against an opponent's subminimum opening bid. The balancing bid can be made with a few points less, but clearly there is no request for the minors here.

How about

RHO	YOU	
2♡	3 NT	or

LHO	PARTNER	RHO	YOU
2♡	Pass	3♡	3 NT?

Since 3 NT is game, it is almost always a natural bid. On both of these auctions, it is very plausible that one is willing to play in game, especially since neither opponent has advertised much strength.

Here are some other 3 NT overcalls to consider:

RHO	YOU	RHO	YOU	RHO	YOU
1♣	3 NT,	1♡	3 NT,	3♣	3 NT,

RHO	YOU	LHO	PARTNER	RHO	YOU
3♡	3 NT,	3♡	Pass	Pass	3 NT

All of these are natural. It isn't surprising for the 3 NT bidder to have a running suit, but 3 NT on these auctions is always an attempt to play it there. On the other hand, here are a few "unusual" 3 NT bids:

LHO	PARTNER	RHO	YOU
1♡	Pass	3♡	3 NT

and

RHO	YOU	LHO	PARTNER
1♡	2♣	2♠	Pass
3♣	3 NT		

It is illogical that you could want to play 3 NT opposite the strong auctions listed above. On the first example, you must be suggesting a sacrifice with something like.

♠ 8   ♡ A   ◇ K Q J 10 6   ♣ Q 10 7 6 4 2.

The second auction cannot show 5–5 or so in the minors since you would have bid 2 NT at your first turn. Since clubs are presumably your longest suit, you would tend to have something like

♠ 8   ♡ K 7   ◇ K Q J 5   ♣ A Q 10 8 7 4,

where you would prefer that partner decided whether to compete in clubs or diamonds. Even a hand like

♠ –   ♡ 10   ◇ A Q 7 6 5   ♣ A J 9 8 7 4 2

is conceivable.

Our analysis of notrump auctions is almost complete. Of course we will need to practice our responses to the unusual notrump, in addition to considering a defense to it. It will be comforting, though, to know that we are now easily aware of what's unusual and what isn't.

Consider 1♠–Pass–4♠–4 NT. This is clearly unusual, but it is unfair to restrict it specifically to the minors. Bid 4 NT in this auction with

♠ 8   ♡ A Q 10 6 4   ◇ A K 8 7 5 3   ♣ 9

and prepare to bid 5◇ over 5♣ and force partner to decide between the red suits.

The auction 3♡–4 NT would be for the minors. What else could you do with

♠ 8   ♡ 6   ◇ A K 7 4 3   ♣ K Q 8 6 4 2?

I would pass with

♠ 9 4   ♡ 8   ◇ K Q 10 6 3   ♣ A Q 10 7 4

but would bid 5♣ with

♠ 9   ♡ –   ◇ K J 7 4 3   ♣ A K Q 10 9 6 3

and double with

♠ A 9 7   ♡ 9   ◇ A Q 9 3   ♣ A J 10 4 3

Double doesn't say that I have discovered a plethora of hearts, it just shows a lot of defense and allows partner to pass or pull based on his hand.

Questions on Unusual NT

Question: **My partner wanted to use a 1 NT overcall vs. two bidding opponents as unusual, showing a light takeout double in the unbid suits. Is that reasonable?**

Answer: Definitely yes, in fact it is my own strong preference. I have never seen the need to play 1 NT as natural after 1◇ – Pass – 1♡ – ? since I never get dealt a strong NT here. And I wouldn't be too anxious to make the bid even if I picked up one, since partner is odds on to have a virtual Yarborough anyway. I would bid 1 NT vulnerable with

♠ J 10 7 4 3   ♡ 8   ◇ A 6   ♣ Q J 7 5 4

where I want to compete, but don't have enough high cards to double, and not enough courage for 2 NT. At favorable vulnerability, 5 – 4's are also quite acceptable for 1 NT in my book.

Question: **What should an overcall of 4 NT be? Is 1♡ – 4 NT an unusual NT?**

Answer: It certainly seems unusual to me! Yes, I would play that as lots of minors, at least 6 – 6.

Question: **You said that if the opponents double an unusual NT, 4th hand should basically ignore it and do whatever he would have. But what should redouble mean?**

Answer: Larry Cohen and I came up with the following, which we use whenever an artificial two-suiter has been doubled:

Pass shows no preference, presumably equal length. *Bids* indicate preferences, which are also lead directing.

Therefore redouble promises a preference, warning against partner leading it unless he has a good sequence of his own. So, after 1♠ – 2NT – Dbl – ? pass with

♠ A 7 4 3   ♡ 6 4 3   ◇ 8 5 2   ♣ 9 7 3.

Bid 3◇ with

♠ A 7 4 3   ♡ 6 4 3 2   ◇ K J 9   ♣ 8 5.

Redouble with

♠ A 7 4 3   ♡ 6 4 3 2   ◇ 8 5   ♣ 6 3 2,

intending to pass after partner pulls to 3♣ (as he must, since my preference could be for clubs). There are clearly other possibilities for redouble, but we have been quite happy with the above.

Question: **What does this auction mean?**

$$1\,\heartsuit \qquad 2\,\text{NT} \qquad \text{Pass} \qquad 3\,\clubsuit$$
$$\text{Pass} \qquad 3\,\spadesuit$$

Answer: 3 ♠ should show a very good hand with three spades as well as 5 – 5 in the minors.

♠ A 7 4   ♡ –   ◇ K Q J 10 9   ♣ A Q J 10 6

feels right for this sequence. Partner can jump to 5 ♣ with

♠ 8 3   ♡ 9 7 5 3   ◇ 8 6 4   ♣ K 9 8 3,

sign off in 4 ♣ with

♠ J 8 6 3   ♡ Q 7 5 3   ◇ 8 3   ♣ 9 7 4,

or even bid 4 ♠ with

♠ K Q 10 6 3   ♡ Q 7 4 2   ◇ 3   ♣ 9 5 4.

Question: **Does the 4 ◇ bid invite a save on this auction? Or is it merely trying to push the opponents one level too high?**

$$1\,\heartsuit \qquad 2\,\text{NT} \qquad 3\,\heartsuit \qquad 4\,\diamondsuit$$
$$4\,\heartsuit$$

Answer: I can see good arguments for both points using standard methods. However, you may like the following, which was conceived by Ethan Stein and me. On auctions where we have bid one or two minors preemptively, a competitive 3 NT (which could hardly be natural) suggests a save in five of a minor. So we would play 4 ◇ as not save-suggesting, since that hand would bid 3 NT.

Responding to Unusual Notrump

When your partner has employed the Unusual Notrump, you should keep in mind that a moderate two-suiter has been shown – usually 5-5. (You should always play an Unusual Notrump bidder to have 5-5, except in the balancing seat where 5-4 or even 4-4 occurs more often.)

You are the captain of these auctions, so don't expect partner to move – he's already shown his hand. Try these responding hands after

LHO	PARTNER	RHO	YOU
1 ♡	2 NT	Pass	?

with neither side vulnerable.

1.   ♠ Q 7 5   ♡ K 9 8 7 4   ◇ Q 6   ♣ 4 3 2

Bid 3 ♣. You were asked to indicate your longer minor.

2.   ♠ K Q J 10 7 4   ♡ 9 5 4 3   ◇ K 6   ♣ 8

Bid 3 ♠. With an independent suit, you can overrule partner.

3.   ♠ K J 10 9   ♡ K Q 10 9 6   ◇ 6 4   ♣ 8 5

Pass. You don't like to do this, but this hand should be practically worthless in three of a minor.

4.   ♠ A 5   ♡ 9 6 5 3   ◇ 8 7 4   ♣ K 10 9 8

Bid 4♣, which should be preemptive. With an invitational hand, you can cuebid. The opponents must have a big spade fit.

5.   ♠ A Q 7 3   ♡ 9 6 3   ◇ A J 7 3   ♣ 9 2

Bid 3♡, which shows interest in game, usually with a fit in one of the minors. Your next bid will be 4◇, inviting game.

6.   ♠ 9   ♡ 6 3 2   ◇ A J 10 7 5   ♣ A 9 8 4

Bid 5◇. It's surprising that the opponents have done so little so far, with their tremendous fits in the majors. You are clearly going to want to be 5◇ eventually, so do it now before the opponents get together. Of course with the magnificent fit, you would not be surprised to make 5◇.

If RHO doubles 2 NT, that doesn't really change things. We would do exactly the same with the above hands.

How big a part does vulnerability play in contemplating an Unusual Notrump bid? It is quite relevant, of course, but you cannot be afraid to bid because you are vulnerable.

Just as with a preempt, when a hand calls for an opening 3–bid, you should select that call without worrying unduly about how much you'll go for if you are doubled and partner tables a Yarborough. Of course, when you are vulnerable, you tend to pass up some frisky bids with indifferent suits that you would risk at favorable vulnerability. After

RHO	YOU
1♡	?

bid 2 NT with unfavorable vulnerability on

        ♠ 9 6   ♡ 8   ◇ A Q 10 9 6   ♣ K J 10 9 4

but pass with

        ♠ 9 6   ♡ 8   ◇ A Q 7 4 2   ♣ K J 6 5 3,

possibly balancing later.

Can an Unusual Notrump bidder ever take further action? Since an Unusual Notrump is a type of preempt, he should be reluctant to do so, but since there is a wide range of strength possible, the situation is different from an opening 2 or 3 bid. After

1♡	2 NT	Dbl	3♣
4♡	?		

it is OK to bid 5♣ with

        ♠ x   ♡ –   ◇ A x x x x x   ♣ K Q J x x x.

The Negative Double

Negative doubles have become one of the most popular of all conventions, and players at all levels are eagerly employing it. It is possible that it is now the third most widely used convention, next to the two old standbys, Stayman and Blackwood.

However, while the popularity of negative doubles has increased dramatically, the same cannot be said about understanding and agreement on it. Not only is this easy to observe with average players, but this confusion can even be seen each month in the comments of the panelists in the "Master Solvers' Club" of *The Bridge World.* Each time a problem is presented involving negative doubles, the panel finds itself sharply divided as to what the right action is. In his book *Bridge Conventions,* Eddie Kantar states that ". . . no two expert partnerships play negative doubles alike."

So what does a negative double show, and when should it be used? A negative double is used by responder after his partner's opening bid has been overcalled. It shows at least a minimum response (6 – 7 or more), but denies the length or strength needed in order for responder to bid a suit of his own.

Here are a few examples of negative doubles after partner's 1 ♣ opening bid has been overcalled with 1 ♠.

1.   ♠ 8 6 4   ♡ A K 5 2   ◇ Q 8 7   ♣ 8 6 4

The negative double of one major always guarantees four or more cards in the other major.

2.   ♠ 9 4   ♡ A J 7 4   ◇ K 3   ♣ 9 8 6 4 3

You could raise clubs, but first you want to check out hearts, just as you would without the overcall. You can raise clubs later, if necessary.

3.   ♠ 8 4   ♡ A Q 9 6 4 3   ◇ 10 7 2   ♣ 9 6

Your suit is good enough to bid, but you shouldn't make a forcing bid at the two level with only 6 points. You will bid your hearts next, showing a hand not strong enough to bid at the two level initially.

One of the reasons for the popularity of negative doubles is the current trend toward five-card majors. Without negative doubles it can become virtually impossible to locate a 4 – 4 major suit fit. This is particularly true if the overcall is in spades and the fit is in hearts, since a bid by responder shows five-card length. This is the reason that negative doubles emphasize the unbid major or majors.

How does opener rebid after the negative double? Since partner has promised at least four in the unbid major, opener tends to bid just as he would if there had been no overcall and partner had directly responded in the major. In other words, opener treats

	1♣	1♠	Dbl	Pass

just like

	1♣	Pass	1♡	Pass,

with one exception. Since there is now a cuebid available, all game forcing sequences begin with it, so that

	1♢	1♠	Dbl	Pass
	3♣			

is invitational, rather than game forcing as

	1♢	Pass	1♡	Pass
	3♣			

would be.

Let's look at some hands in order to see how to respond to the negative double.

The auction has been:

	1♢	1♠	Dbl	Pass

1.   ♠ J 7   ♡ 6 2   ♢ K Q J 10 6 4   ♣ A Q 4

Bid 2♢ – just what you would have bid if partner had responded 1♡.

2.   ♠ A 5   ♡ K 6 4 3   ♢ K Q 8 5 4   ♣ K 3
Bid 3♡ for the same reason as in (1).

3.   ♠ A 6 3   ♡ 9   ♢ K Q J 10 4   ♣ A K 7 3
Bid 3♣, invitational. If your hand were a little better you would cuebid 2♠ in order to force to game.

What do you do with a hand worth a penalty double? For example, you hold:

♠ A Q 10 6 4   ♡ K 8 6 3   ♢ 9   ♣ J 8 3

and partner's 1♢ opening bid is overcalled with 1♠. You must now pass and hope partner can reopen with a double. He will do so whenever his opening bid includes spade shortness or he has a good hand. The higher the level of the overcall, however, the less likely partner is to reopen unless he has extra values. Therefore with

♠ A J 7 4   ♡ K 6 3   ♢ 8 5   ♣ A Q 7 2

after 1♢ – 2♠ bid 3 NT rather than passing since partner may not be able to take any more action.

How high should negative doubles be played? Some people claim that they play them through 7♠, although at the higher levels the double is usually left in by opener. The philosophy of these players is that when an opponent jumps to game, his suit will be good enough so that responder is unlikely to have enough of a trump stack to make a pure penalty double. Most players play negative doubles through 2 or 3♠, but it is advisable for the partnership to make its own decisions here.

Next we will continue our look at negative doubles by answering commonly asked questions regarding them.

Questions and Answers on Negative Doubles

Here are some questions that I've often been asked about negative doubles which might also clarify this topic for the reader.

Question: **If 1♣-1♡ [overcall]-Dbl shows four spades, does 1♣-1♡-1♠ show five?**

Answer: Yes, most people play it this way, so opener can raise freely with 3-card support.

Question: **Does 1♣-1◊-Dbl show both majors? Also, what about 1◊-2♣-Dbl and 1♣-2◊-Dbl?**

Answer: 1♣-1◊-Dbl does show at least 4 cards in each major, since responder can easily bid his major at the one level, holding just one of them. However, the other sequences cannot guarantee both majors. The requirements for bidding a new suit at the two level are stricter, since it shows five and a pretty good hand.

Question: **What does an auction like 1♡-1♠-Dbl show?**

Answer: It usually shows both minors but responder might have

♠ 8 4   ♡ 7 3   ◊ K 8 7 5 3 2   ♣ A J 6

where he is really not strong enough for 2◊.

Question: **Is 1♣-1♡-Dbl-Pass,-2♠ a strong bid?**

Answer: If you remember that opener treats the negative double here as if responder had bid 1♠ without an overcall, it can't be too strong. But since 1♠ is available for weaker hands, 2♠ should show 15-16 points in support of spades. With 17-19 points, opener should jump to 3♠ to strongly invite game.

Question: **If responder makes a negative double, and then later doubles the same suit again, is the second double for penalties?**

Answer: since a negative double is a type of takeout double, these situations are the same:

1◊	Dbl	Pass	1♠
2◊	Dbl		

1◊	1♠	Dbl	2♠
Pass	Pass	Dbl	

The second double simply says that you have sufficient values to compete further.

Question: **Do you ever make a negative double on a good hand?**

Answer: With an unbalanced hand it is usually not necessary, since you can afford to bid your suits. After 1◊-1♠ you bid 2♣ on

♠ A 7   ♡ A Q 6 3   ◊ 6 4   ♣ K Q 7 5 2

and bid the hearts next. An exception can be made when the auction is already at a high level. You would negative double with

♠ A Q 7 4   ♡ Q 5   ◊ 9 3   ♣ A K 7 6 3

after 1♡ by partner and a 3◊ overcall since, after 4♣, it would be impossible to get to 3 NT and very difficult to get to 4♠. It is common, though, to negative double on a good balanced hand, where you don't want to emphasize any suit of your own. You should double after 1 ◊ by partner, 1 ♠ overcall with

♠ J 8 4　　♡ A Q 7 3　　◊ A 5 4　　♣ K 9 4

since you can't bid a suit of your own. You will next cuebid to show your strength.

Question: **When should you pass partner's negative double?**

Answer: At high levels (3 or 4) you tend to pass with balanced hands when you have no obvious bid, since partner needs a pretty good hand to double you should be able to get a plus score. At lower levels you need good trumps to pass, since you will be attempting to hold declarer to very few tricks, and his trumps are located behind yours.

Question: **What does an auction like the following show?**

1 ◊	1 ♠	Pass	2 ♠
Pass	Pass	Dbl	

or

1 ◊	1 ♠	Pass	Pass
2 ♣	2 ♠	Dbl	

Answer: This shows a hand which wanted to make a penalty double the first time. Opener should therefore virtually always leave this double in.

Question: **Can negative doubles be used after partner's opening bid in NT has been overcalled?**

Answer: The great majority of players do not use negative doubles in this situation. However, it is plausible to play them here also, particularly against opponents who have their bid when overcalling. Certainly a negative double is the only good solution after 1 NT - 2 ◊ and you hold

♠ Q 7 6 3　　♡ Q 7 6 2　　◊ 8　　♣ J 5 4 3.

Some players already use negative doubles on auctions like 1 NT - 3 ♡, since the 3 ♡ bidder must have a good long suit for his bid.

Question: **Is there anything special that you must do when your opponents are using negative doubles?**

Answer: The best way to answer that is by examining a sequence like

1 ◊	1 ♠	Dbl	?

and seeing what effect the double would have on the various calls.

PASS: Since partner will have another chance, it is not necessary to bid on borderline hands unless you have trump support. Also, even with spade shortness, you shouldn't be overly concerned about the double being left in, since it is not easy for opener to pass the double.

1 NT or 2 ♣: These mean exactly the same as if responder hadn't doubled.

2 ◊: The cuebid guarantees spade support since you could redouble on a good hand without support.

2 ♡: Remember that responder has promised at least four hearts. It probably isn't necessary to play this as a cuebid, but if you do bid it naturally you'd better have a real good suit.

2 ♠: This has the same meaning as if responder had passed, except that

the minimum requirement for the bid is slightly less because of the competitive aspects of the hand, just like

$$1 \spadesuit \qquad Dbl \qquad 2 \spadesuit$$

may be bid with slightly less than

$$1 \spadesuit \qquad Pass \qquad 2 \spadesuit .$$

2 NT: Some players use this as a limit raise, just like

$$1 \spadesuit \qquad Dbl \qquad 2 \; NT$$

since you would redouble with lots of high cards.

REDOUBLE: This shows a good hand interested in penalizing the opponents and tends to deny spade support.

Negative doubles are certainly here to stay, but there is definitely more to them than you might have been led to believe. As with many other sequences, the key to success is discussion, understanding, and agreement between players.

Question: **What would you do holding**

$$\spadesuit K\,6\,5 \qquad \heartsuit 10\,5\,3 \qquad \diamondsuit 8\,7\,4 \qquad \clubsuit A\,Q\,9\,5$$

after 1 ◊ – 1 ♡ ? Is a negative double plausible?

Answer: Obviously there is no good choice on this hand. Pass seems wrong when your side owns the balance of strength and you have such a weak holding in the opponent's suit. The best method for this particular hand would be to play that a negative double here shows only three spades since you could bid them with four or more. As you may remember I reported that most people played 1 ♣ – 1 ♡ – Dbl as showing four, with 1 ♠ promising five. This is still the way most people play it, but there are some who play that the negative double here truly shows that you don't have a good bid. Even playing that a double shows four spades here I would make that call, believing that it is the lesser of evils.

Question: **Does this auction show extra values by the opener or is it merely competitive?**

$$1 \spadesuit \qquad 2 \diamondsuit \qquad Dbl \qquad 3 \diamondsuit$$
$$4 \clubsuit$$

Answer: As commonly played, the negative double guarantees four or more hearts here, but clubs are not guaranteed. Responder could certainly have made a negative double holding

$$\spadesuit K\,8 \qquad \heartsuit Q\,8\,4\,3\,2 \qquad \diamondsuit 6\,5\,4 \qquad \clubsuit K\,J\,5,$$

so opener needs quite a good hand to venture to the four level in a suit that his partner may not fit. On the other hand, a bid of 3 ♡ after

$$1 \spadesuit \qquad 2 \diamondsuit \qquad Dbl \qquad 3 \diamondsuit$$

doesn't show that much, since responder has guaranteed possession of hearts.

Question: **What does this auction show?**

$$1 \spadesuit \qquad 2 \diamondsuit \qquad Dbl \qquad Pass$$
$$2 \heartsuit \qquad Pass \qquad 2 \spadesuit$$

Answer: This is an unusual auction which should sound strange to the naked ear. Responder has shown hearts, yet when opener bids them, he retreats back to spades, a suit he could have raised in the first place. The only type hand that really makes any sense is one like

♠ 8 4 2   ♡ A Q 6   ◇ 7 4 3   ♣ K Q 6 5,

where responder is too good to bid 2♠ but doesn't really want to force to the three level with such bad trumps.

Question: **Is there a point-count limit for negative doubles?**

Answer: There is no upper limit for negative doubles since they depend on and are related to distribution more than point count. Notice that this is also true for takeout doubles. As for the lower limit, at the one level it is the usual six points while for each higher level you need at least two extra points.

Question: **If you are playing negative doubles, does this auction show a five-card suit?**

	Opp	
1♣	1◇	1♠

Answer: I don't play it that way, since I play that the double of 1◇ guarantees both majors. However, it is only fair to point out that many people do play that 1♠ shows five.

Question: **The auction has gone**

NORTH	EAST	SOUTH	WEST
1◇	1♠	Dbl	3♠
Pass	Pass	Dbl	

Is South's second double on this auction for penalties, takeout, or cooperative? Also, how much strength does it show?

Answer: If 3♠ was a *limit* raise, then it is unlikely that you would want to double the opponents for penalties below game. Also, since the first double was for "takeout," the subsequent double could not show a spade stack. I would consider this to be a second "takeout" double, showing something like

♠ 8   ♡ A 10 6 4   ◇ K 7 3   ♣ K 8 7 4 2.

Of course, partner may choose to leave it in if he has spades.

If 3♠ was a *preemptive* raise, then the double would not be "cooperative." Partner would leave this double in more frequently since the 3♠ bidder has a weak hand. The doubler should have at least 10 high card points.

Question: **What does a redouble of a negative double show?**

Answer: The standard meaning of a redouble on an auction like

NORTH	EAST	SOUTH	WEST
1◇	1♠	Dbl	Redbl

is that West has a good hand, usually without trump support. West would like partner to double the opponent's next call if feasible, bid the obvious with a very distributional hand, or pass the opponent's call around to the redoubler. Notice that this parallels the meaning of redouble on an auction like

1♡	Dbl	Redbl

However, a concept that has gained support recently is that since fourth hand is unlikely to have a good hand with three people bidding, the redouble should be used conventionally for a more practical consideration. Dr. George Rosenkranz suggested that in both

	1◇	1♠	Dbl	Redbl
and				
	1♡	1♠	2♣	Dbl

the last call could more profitably be used to show a high honor in partner's suit. This kind of hand obviously *does* occur often, and is invaluable on defense and for directing opening leads.

The negative inference is also valuable, since the failure to redouble would usually deny a high honor. If you choose to play the redouble this way, write "negative redouble" on your card under "other." You must be careful about levels, however, since the opponents may let you play in your redoubled contract at the two or three level!

Question: **I have questions about two hands where I made negative doubles after partner opened 1♣ and next hand overcalled 1♠. In both cases we were playing matchpoints, with neither side vulnerable. These were the hands:**

1.   ♠ –   ♡ A K J 9   ◇ A K 10 6 4   ♣ K 9 3 2

and

2.   ♠ A 6   ♡ K 10 7 6 4 3   ◇ 9 6 3   ♣ 10 5.

In each case I came in for a good deal of criticism.

Answer: Let's take the second hand first, since the alternatives are less complicated. After 1♣ – 1♠, our options are Pass, Double, 2♡, and 3♡ (preemptive). 2♡ is forcing and suggests a rebid, which is more bidding than this mediocre hand should do. Pass seems unduly conservative, with 1½ quick tricks and a six-card suit. 3♡ shows six with a modest hand (as long as we are playing weak jump shifts in competition), but I would like to have a better suit when going to the three level. Therefore, I would also negative double with this hand – admittedly an imperfect call, but I hope to get the chance to bid 2♡ at my next turn.

Of course, a nonforcing 2♡ (negative-free bid) would be just perfect for all the right reasons. (Of course, if too many of my opponents started using the good methods that I write about, it would be a lot more difficult to win!)

Your negative double on hand (1) is certainly the strongest that I have ever seen. However, that does not make it wrong. A negative double does not have an upper point-count limit, and later we will be able to cuebid spades to show our good hand, even though partner will tend not to play us for this much the first time around.

Your alternative action is presumably 2◇, since no jump bid would suggest the three-suited nature of the hand, and most experienced players would use the cuebid as a club raise denying four hearts. Partner would not know of your hearts after 2◇, and it might be awkward to reach a heart contract.

Since the game is matchpoints, we certainly would like to play in hearts if partner has four of them. I would bid 2 ◇ in standard, but my second choice is double, and I certainly don't believe that your choice was nuts.

Question: **I recently held**

♠ 6 4   ♡ A Q   ◇ K 10 5 4   ♣ A 9 7 4 2

and opened 1 ♣. My LHO overcalled with 1 ♠ and my partner doubled, which I Alerted as negative. After RHO passed, I rebid 2 ◇. My partner then proceded to get us too high and told me later that I had "reversed." In the process of setting him straight, I may have said a few things that I shouldn't have. At least, I was correct, wasn't I?

Answer: I assume that you are asking whether you were correct in that your auction didn't promise a reverse, not whether you were correct in saying things to your partner that you shouldn't have. (The answer to that is obviously *No.*)

I do treat 2 ◇ as a reverse, for two reasons. My negative doubles of 1 ♠ merely promise hearts, not necessarily a second suit. I would always negative double 1 ♠ with

♠ A 5 2   ♡ K 10 9 5   ◇ 7 6 3   ♣ J 5 3 or

♠ 10 8 7 3   ♡ K J 8 6   ◇ Q 9 3   ♣ Q 6,

and would not relish getting to 2 ◇ or 3 ♣ opposite the aforementioned

♠ 6 4   ♡ A Q   ◇ K 8 5 4   ♣ A 9 7 4 2.

Also, I regard 1 ♣ – 1 ♠ – Dbl as the same beginning as 1 ♣ – Pass – 1 ♡, in that 2 ♡ by opener is just a raise, while 2 ◇ is a big bid, since responder never promised diamonds and it is higher ranking than opener's first bid suit.

However, my 2 ◇ reverse is non-forcing in this auction! I play that after an opponent's overcall, the only forcing bid is a cuebid of the opponent's suit. All jumps, including jump shifts, as well as reverses, promise extra values, but are passable. I would bid 2 ◇ on this auction with

♠ 9 3   ♡ A Q   ◇ K J 9 7   ♣ A Q 8 5 4,

but with another ace, make a game-forcing bid of 2 ♠.

However, in my discussions with other top players, I am quite aware that most of them would not treat

1 ♣	1 ♠	Dbl	Pass
2 ◇			

as a reverse and would happily bid exactly as you did – though some of them would open 1 ◇ rather than 1 ♣ with your hand.

The real answer to this (and many other questions involving negative doubles) is that the only way to ensure that you and your partner share the same opinion is to talk it over.

Question: **Holding**

♠ Q J 7 4   ♡ 8   ◇ K Q J 6 5   ♣ 9 7 2

what should I have done after

Pass	Pass	1 ◇	3 ♣
?			

Answer: You want to play 4 ♠ if partner has four, so make a negative double, which does not promise both majors here. If partner makes the expected heart response, you will correct to diamonds.

Responsive Doubles

Many years ago, bridge players decided it was impractical to use an immediate seat double of an opening bid for penalties. Thus was born one of the first bridge conventions – the takeout double.

Many years later, it was suggested that 1 ♣ –1 ♠ –Dbl was also somewhat impractical to use as a business double and, as a result, negative doubles were introduced. Only a short time later, theoreticians decided it didn't make sense to treat a double as business when the opponents bid and raised the same suit. So the responsive double came into being.

When do we use the responsive double? Although its use has been expanded, the basic responsive double action is something like this:

Opener	Partner	Responder	You
1 ♡	Dbl	2 ♡	?

and your hand is:

♠ A 5 3   ♡ 8 7   ◇ Q 8 7 5   ♣ Q 9 4 2.

You have enough to compete, but it is far from obvious which suit your partnership should compete in. If you guess a minor you could easily guess the wrong one, and it would be presumptuous to bid spades holding only three. The answer is to make a counter takeout double. You can now abide by partner's decision, even if he bids spades. He will assume that you would have bid them with four, so to bid spades he will need five or a very good four.

Here is another perfect responsive double hand – the auction has proceeded

Opener	Partner	Responder	You
1 ♣	Dbl	2 ♣	?

and you have

♠ K 7 4   ♡ Q 8 3   ◇ 7 6 4 3   ♣ A 5 2.

Once again it can't be right to sell out at a low level, but your only four-card suit is a weak minor and there might easily be a better spot, opposite something like

♠ A 6 5 3   ♡ A J 7 4 2   ◇ K 5 2   ♣ 8,

which is certainly a normal takeout double.

At the table, of course, you probably will not be dealt these perfect hand-types. It is perfectly all right to use the responsive double on these hands also, as long as you restrict its use to the hands where you really are on a guess. If you hold

$$\spadesuit\ K\,Q\,7\,4 \qquad \heartsuit\ Q\,8\,3 \qquad \diamond\ 6\,4 \qquad \clubsuit\ J\,7\,5\,4$$

after

Opener	Partner	Responder	You
1 ◇	Dbl	2 ◇	?

you should bid 2 ♠, since that is likely to be your side's best spot. In addition, spades are what you want led if you wind up defending a diamond contract.

The strength shown by a responsive double is limited, showing about 6–11 high-card points depending on the level. You can double after 1 ♠ –Dbl–2 ♠ with a pretty weak hand, since you are forcing partner to bid only at the two-level. On the other hand, after 1 ♠ –Dbl–2 ♠ you need a little more since partner will have to bid a suit at the three-level. The responsibility for competing lies with the partner of the takeout doubler, since the doubler has already shown his strength. Therefore, it is better for responder to borrow a point if necessary than for the doubler to double again without extra values.

With more than 11 highs or with better distribution, it is still right to cuebid to tell partner of your great strength immediately. Otherwise the opponents might crowd the auction and prevent you from showing your extra values.

In all our examples, the responsive double has taken place after partner has made a takeout double and responder has raised his partner's suit. What happens if responder bids a suit of his own or notrump? Should a double by fourth hand still be responsive? Although there are times when it might work out better, the answer is no. A double is not responsive when the opponents have not yet agreed on a suit. Therefore, with

$$\spadesuit\ 8\,5 \qquad \heartsuit\ K\,J\,7\,4 \qquad \diamond\ K\,J\,6\,2 \qquad \clubsuit\ 10\,6\,3$$

bid 2♡ after

$$1\spadesuit\ -\text{Dbl}-1\spadesuit\ -?\ \text{or}\ 1\spadesuit\ -\text{Dbl}-1\text{NT}-?$$

One reason that this is necessary is to expose a psych. If 1♡ –Dbl–1♠ –Dbl is responsive, what could you do with

$$\spadesuit\ A\,J\,7\,4\,3 \qquad \heartsuit\ A\,5\,4 \qquad \diamond\ 6\,5 \qquad \clubsuit\ 7\,4\,3$$

on the above auction if the double didn't show spades? The opponents would be able to talk you out of your spade fit unless you could expose their possible psych by doubling.

How high should responsive doubles be used? This can be left to the discretion of each partnership, but the most popular levels are through 3 ◇, 3 ♠ or 4♡. At the higher levels, of course, the double tends to be left in fairly often whether responsive or not, just as with negative doubles.

Another similarity to negative doubles is the way that the partner of the doubler bids in response. After 1 ◇ –Dbl–2 ◇ –Dbl, the original doubler will usually make a minimum bid in the appropriate suit, but can jump to show extra values and invite game. A cuebid remains the only force. Try bidding the following hands in response to partner's responsive double after the auction has begun

Opener	You	Responder	Partner
1♡	Dbl	2♡	Dbl
Pass	?		

1) ♠ A 7 4 3 Bid 3◊. If partner had spades he would have bid them.
   ♡ 8 5
   ◊ A K 6 2
   ♣ Q 9 4

2) ♠ A 10 6 5 Bid 4◊. This is quite a good hand but you can't be sure of
   ♡ 9   game, so an invitational bid is sufficient. Don't hang part-
   ◊ A Q J 9 3 ner for competing.
   ♣ A J 4

3) ♠ A K Q 5 Bid 2♠. With your strong spades you are willing to play a
   ♡ 8 7   4–3 fit, and you would prefer to remain at the two-level
   ◊ A 7 4   with this minimum hand.
   ♣ 10 6 4 3

4) ♠ A Q 5 4 Bid 3♡. This time you are strong enough to commit the
   ♡ –   hand to game.
   ◊ A J 7 6 5
   ♣ A Q 8 4

Responsive doubles are also commonly played after your partner doubles a weak two-bid, assuming that you play responsive doubles high enough. After 2♠–Dbl–3♠ you would double with

♠ 9 5   ♡ A 6 3   ◊ K 10 5 4   ♣ K 10 6 3,

since you are prepared for any action partner wishes to take.

If responder jump raises his partner's opening bid, there is still no reason not to use responsive doubles. Since the auction is already at the three-level, you must have reasonably good values to compete at this level.

Although responsive doubles were originally intended for auctions after a takeout double, most good players also employ them after overcalls, provided the opponents have agreed on a suit. Thus double would be responsive on each of these auctions:

		Partner		You
1)	1♡	1♠	3♡	Dbl
2)	1♣	1♡	3♣	Dbl
3)	1♣	1♡	2♣	Dbl
4)	2♠	3◊	3♠	Dbl

These doubles show the other two suits and tend to deny support for partner's suit, since you would then be in a position to raise him. After

	Partner		You
1 ◇	1 ♠	2 ◇	?

you would double with

♠ 8 6   ♡ A K 7 4   ◇ 8 3   ♣ Q J 7 5 2

which partner could even leave in with

♠ A Q 8 7 4   ♡ J 5 3   ◇ A J 9 4   ♣ 10

Try these hands on the auction

	Partner		You
1 ♡	2 ◇	2 ♡	?

1) ♠ Q J 10 9 4   Bid 2 ♠. Your spades are good enough to bid freely.
    ♡ A 5
    ◇ 9 3
    ♣ K 7 5 4

2) ♠ K J 5   Bid 3 ◇. You really don't want to force partner to bid one
    ♡ 6 5 4 3   of your anemic black suits, and your diamond holding
    ◇ A J   is certainly powerful enough to allow you to compete in
    ♣ 10 7 4 3   in the suit. Also, you would like a diamond lead if you
                 wind up defending 3 ♡.

3) ♠ 10 5 4 3   Bid 2 NT. This hand is certainly worth inviting game
    ♡ A Q 7   in NT.
    ◇ A 5
    ♣ 9 7 4 2

4) ♠ J 10 8 7 5   Double. You would prefer to have a second diamond in
    ♡ A 4   case partner rebids those, but the hand is otherwise per-
    ◇ 9   fectly suited to a responsive double.
    ♣ K Q 7 4 3

Is it ever possible to make a penalty double when the opponents have bid
and raised a suit below the level of your responsive double?

Usually not, except when they balance up to the three level on an auction
like:

You		Partner	
1 ♣	1 ♡	2 ♣	Dbl
Pass	2 ◇	Pass	Pass
3 ♣	Dbl		

This definitely means that you would like to try for blood.

Can the responsive double theme be extended even further? Yes, it can.
Many pairs now play that any time the opponents bid and raise a suit (particularly at the two level) the double is responsive. This group would treat all
of the following as responsive doubles:

	Partner		You
1 ♡	1 NT	2 ♡	Dbl

You		Partner	
1♣	1♡	1♠	2♡
Dbl			

1♣	1♡	Dbl*	2♡
Dbl			

Partner		You	
1♣	1♡	Dbl*	2♡
Pass	Pass	Dbl	

(*Neg.)

There is even a case for treating this double as responsive:

1♣	Pass	1♡	Dbl
2♣	2♠	Dbl	

since the opponents have agreed on a suit, in effect bidding and raising spades.

To avoid possible misunderstandings, my partners and I agree to play that when the opponents bid and raise a suit, all doubles through 3♢ are responsive. Therefore, we are never in doubt as to partner's intent.

Support Doubles

Any experienced player will tell you that showing support for partner's major suit is vitally important. This becomes especially crucial in competitive auctions.

However, "support" can be a relative term. You open 1♣ and the auction proceeds:

$$1♣ -Pass-1♡ -2♢ -$$

back to you. Everyone would raise to 2♡ holding

♠ 9 5   ♡ A K Q 7   ◇ 8 4   ♣ K 9 6 4 3.

But would you also bid 2♡ with

♠ A Q 6 5   ♡ Q 8 5   ◇ J 7   ♣ K J 6 4 ?

Any player worth his salt would.

How can partner judge what to do holding something like

♠ 8 7 4   ♡ 9 6 4 3   ◇ A 3 2   ♣ A Q 7

when the bidding goes:

	YOU		PARTNER	
	1♣	Pass	1♡	2♢
	2♡	3♢	?	

Opposite the first hand you will probably make 4♡ or 5♡ (although game may not be biddable), yet opposite the second hand you are too high at 3♡. The difference between three and four-card support can be overwhelming.

The following solution to this problem has been gaining some adherents among the leading players. After

$$1♣-Pass-1♡-2♢$$
$$?$$

for example, we use the double to show three-card support, reserving the 2♡ raise for hands with four-card support.

We do give up the chance to penalize the opponents after an overcall, but such penalty doubles have very low frequency. Since I began playing support doubles, I have not yet lost out on a penalty double. In the meantime there have been numerous opportunities to clarify the trump holding, leading to greater accuracy in part-score and game bidding.

We play support doubles only up to 2-of-responder's-suit, since there is no safety beyond that level. So far we have used them only after responder has bid a major at the one-level, but we may have just begun to scratch the surface as to the possibilities of such doubles.

In each of the following auctions, we would Alert the double as showing exactly three-card support.

a) 1♣-1♢-1♠-2♡
   Dbl

b) 1♢-Pass-1♡-1♠
   Dbl

c) 1♡-Pass-1♠-2♣
   Dbl

d) 1♣-1♢-1♠-2♢
   Dbl

e) 1♣-Dbl-1♡-2♢
   Dbl

f) 1♣-Pass-1♡-2♢
   Dbl

g) 1♣-1♢-1♡-1NT
   Dbl

h) 1♢-1♡-1♠-2♢
   Dbl

Try the following. Vul: None

	YOU		PARTNER	
	1♢	Pass	1♠	2♣
	?			

1) ♠ K Q 6
   ♡ A Q 6 3
   ♢ A 10 7 4 3
   ♣ 8

2) ♠ A Q 10 7
   ♡ 8
   ♢ A K 9 7 4
   ♣ 8 6 4

3) ♠ K 5 4
   ♡ A 7 3
   ♢ A J 8 6 4 2
   ♣ 9

4) ♠ 8 7 4　　5) ♠ A K　　6) ♠ A 6
　 ♡ A Q 6　　　 ♡ A 8 7 4　　 ♡ K 5 3
　 ◇ A K 7 4　　 ◇ K 10 6 3　　 ◇ A J 10 8 6 4
　 ♣ 9 5 3　　　 ♣ 9 5 3　　　 ♣ J 5

7) ♠ A 7
　 ♡ K 5
　 ◇ Q J 8 6 4
　 ♣ A Q 10 6

1) DBL. You have more than a single raise, but the best first move on your hand must be to show three trumps.

2) 3♠. This hand is too good for a single raise, so give the immediate jump to show your strength.

3) DBL. You may get the chance to rebid your diamonds later, but the opportunity to support partner's suit without committing the hand to spades is too good to pass up.

4) DBL. Your spades aren't much to look at, but there are three of them.

5) PASS. This shows fewer than three spades.

6) 2◇. This also denies three spades.

7) PASS. You would like to double for penalties, but every convention or treatment has its awkward hands. Perhaps partner can reopen with a double.

Now that we've seen life from opener's point of view, let's see how responder reacts after a support double.
After the auction:

PARTNER		YOU	
1♣	Dbl	1♡	1♠
Dbl	Pass	?	

what do you do with each of these?

8) ♠ K 10 6　　9) ♠ 8 5　　　10) ♠ 8 7 3 2
　 ♡ K Q 7 3　　 ♡ A J 6 3　　　 ♡ A Q J 9
　 ◇ 8 6 4 3　　 ◇ Q 8 5　　　　 ◇ 6 5
　 ♣ 9 5　　　　 ♣ J 9 6 4　　　 ♣ J 7 3

11) ♠ 9　　　　12) ♠ 9 6　　　13) ♠ 9 5
　 ♡ K J 9 6 5 4 2　 ♡ A Q J 6 5　　 ♡ K Q 9 6 3
　 ◇ 8 6　　　　 ◇ A 4 3　　　　 ◇ K J 8 7 4
　 ♣ K 5 2　　　 ♣ 10 8 5　　　 ♣ 10

8) 1 NT. This seems like as good a contract as any.

9) 2♣. You don't have an eight-card fit in hearts, but maybe you do in clubs.

10) 2♡. You are certainly not afraid to play a 4–3 fit with those hearts.

11) 4♡. A hand like this practically doubles in value when partner supports the long suit, even though it's only with three-card support.

12) 3♡. Invitational. Just as if partner raised to 2♡ and you tried for game.

13) 2♦. How does your hand look opposite a red two-suiter, partner? Partner bids a regressive 2♡ with

♠ Q J 8 5   ♡ J 7 4   ♦ 6   ♣ A K J 6 4,

but should bid his head off with

♠ 10 7 3 2   ♡ A J 5   ♦ A Q   ♣ Q 7 3 2.

When the opponents use a support double against you, is there any way to turn it to your advantage? After

	YOU		
1♣	Pass	1♡	2♦
Dbl	?		

the partner of the overcaller has extra means of showing support. You can raise to 3♦ with

♠ A 6 5 3   ♡ 8 5   ♦ J 10 4   ♣ Q 10 6 3

or raise preemptively to 4♦ with

♠ 10   ♡ 9 6 4   ♦ K Q 10 6   ♣ 10 8 7 5 3.

However, you now can also redouble to show a top diamond honor (a la Rosenkranz) with

♠ J 10 6 4   ♡ 9 6 4   ♦ A 8   ♣ 8 7 5 3

or cuebid 2♡ with

♠ A 6   ♡ 9 7 3   ♦ A 6 5 4   ♣ Q 9 7 3

to show a limit raise in diamonds. Notice that these last two actions would not have been available if opener had raised to 2♡.

Although the main benefit of support doubles and true support raises occurs when we can discover whether we have the eighth trump or not, it can also be very helpful to pinpoint the nature of our support opposite a five-card suit as well. The ninth trump invariably plays a leading role in the play, particularly from a handling point of view on distributional hands. With the use of support doubles, we can now more accurately judge in the bidding whether partner will be able to trump all of our losers, or merely some of them.

Questions to Clarify Support Doubles

Question: It is obvious that support doubles are alertable. Are there any other alerts that should be given when playing this convention?

Answer: We alert the raise to two as guaranteeing four-card support. We also alert opener's pass or other bid as denying three card support for responder's suit. Although some may believe that alerting passes is extreme (and or silly) it feels right to us since they do convey specific information.

Question: What do you think of support redoubles? Do you play them?

Answer: Yes. Although they don't occur as often as support doubles, they cause me to feel very comfortable when an opponent makes a takeout double after we have bid two suits. All hands with three card support for responder redouble, so raises promise four trump. All other actions show 0–2.

Question: What do you do when playing support redoubles when you have a very strong hand without three card support?

Answer: If you have a good descriptive bid you should make it, otherwise you pass and await developments. The opponents may very well be in trouble, since they are outgunned and may have no fit at all. You will get another chance to bid later, if the opponents fail to bid, you will play in a cozy one heart doubled, probably making overtricks.

Question: Do you and Larry Cohen have any special agreements involving support doubles that may not have yet appeared in print?

Answer: We do play support doubles (and redoubles) after a one diamond response as well as responses in a major. Although the raises promising four trump are rare, we like to be able to show and deny possession of three diamonds.

We also have found it useful to arrive at two agreements to "preempt" when we know that we have a fit. Holding

♠ 8   ♡ K Q 10 6   ◇ 8 6 4   ♣ A Q 10 74

After:

1♣	Pass	1♡	1♠
?			

we bid 3♡, which promises a minimum hand with good distribution, almost always including a singleton or void. Of course we alert this. With a standard invitational 3♡ bid like

♠ A 7   ♡ K 10 8 5   ◇ K 7   ♣ A J 10 6 4

we support double (showing only three trumps) and clarify later. We must include this possibility when we give an explanation for support doubles and redoubles.

Our second special preempt involves action by responder. After opener has made a support double (or redouble). If we jump to three of our original suit, it is also preemptive (competitive). Doesn't that also seem to be the correct tactical action after

1 ◇	Pass	1 ♡	1 ♠
Dbl	2 ♣	?	

Holding

♠ 6 4 2		♠ K	
♡ Q J 10 9 6	or	♡ K 10 7 4 3 2	
◇ K J 7 4		◇ 10 6 4	
♣ 9		♣ 9 5 3	?

Would you really expect to buy the hand for 2♡? Of course, this jump is also very alertable. If responder wants to make a game try, he can either bid a new suit or cue bid (not necessarily game forcing).

Question: Are support doubles still on if the opponents cue bid or bid, NT, regardless of whether their bids are natural or not?

Answer: Yes, our agreement involving support doubles is: They are on below two of responder's suit over *any* interference.

Question: I believe that I understand the basics behind support doubles, but am confused as to how responder proceeds on nonobvious hands. Would you clarify?

Answer: I'll be happy to.
After

1 ◇	Pass	1 ♡	1 ♠
Dbl	Pass	?	

1NT = weak, nonforcing.
2 ♣ = natural, one round force, ambigous length in rounded suits (C + H)
2 ◇ = weak, nonforcing
2 ♡ = weak, usually 5 or 4 good hearts.
2 ♠ at least invitational strength, 5 + hearts. Says nothing about spades.
2 NT = natural, nonforcing, probably only four hearts.
3 ♠ 5-5 in clubs and hearts, not game forcing.
3 ◇ natural, invitational, passable.
3 ♡ = Larry Cohen and I play ths as preemptive, others would say invitational
3 NT = only four hearts, usually passed
4 ♡ = not interested in slam

After

1 ◇	Pass	1 ♡	1 ♠
Dbl	2 ♣	?	

We play good-bad here (see page 112), for others who don't:

Dbl = responsive (cards), usually four hearts
2 NT = invitational, usually four hearts is invitational
3 ♣ = game try promising 5+ hearts, may not be real suit.
3 ♢ = natural, not forcing, could be very weak
3 ♡ = competitive
3 ♠ = game forcing, slam still possible, 5+ hearts
3 NT = usually passed
4 ♢ = natural, forcing, only four hearts
4 ♡ = no slam interest

Question: Is there any alternative to passing when you hold a penalty double but are playing support doubles?

Answer: After

1 ♢	Pass	1 ♡	1 ♠
?			

None vul. I would bid 3 NT with

♠ K Q 7 4   ♡ K   ♢ A K J 10 7   ♣ A 9 4

and 2 ♢ with

♠ A K 8 7   ♡ Q 5   ♢ K J 10 8 7 4   ♣ 9

but most hands should pass and hope that: partner can double, everyone passes and opponents had a better spot, or that we get another chance to penalize them. Losing the opportunity to make a penalty double here has proven to be no more of a problem than giving up penalty doubles after 1 ♣ - 1 ♠.

Question: After support doubling (or redoubling), do you ever pull partner's 3 NT bid.

Answer: I would bid 4 ♣ after

1 ♢	Pass	1 ♡	1 ♠
Dbl	2 ♠	3 NT	Pass
?			

with

♠ —   ♡ A Q 6   ♢ K 9 7 4 2   ♣ A 10 6 4 3

and 4 ♢ with

♠ 9   ♡ A K J   ♢ Q J 10 9 6 4 2   ♣ 8 4.

However unless it was this obvious I would pass and hope for the best. Presumably you should do whatever you would after

1 ♢	Pass	1 ♡	1 ♠
2 ♡	2 ♠	3 NT	Pass
?			

in standard, assuming you feel free to raise hearts here on three.

Question: If I support double (or redouble) with extra values, how do I clarify later?

Answer: By using common sense, based on what partner did. Holding

♠ A J 4   ♡ A K 6   ◇ A 9 7 4 3   ♣ Q 2.

After

1 ◇	Pass	1 ♡	1 ♠
Dbl	Pass	?	

I would rebid 2 NT if partner made a minimum bid like 1 NT, 2 ◇ or 2 ♡. Over any other action I would bid 3 NT. If instead my hand was

♠ 8   ♡ A Q 4   ◇ A Q 9 7 3   ♣ K J 9 6

I would rebid 3 ♣ after partner's minimum rebids. If instead partner made a stronger bid such as 3 ◇ or 2 ♠, I would either bid 4 ♣ or cue bid to let partner know about my extra values.

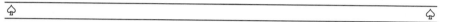

Doubles – After We Open the Bidding

For sophisticated partnerships, there are even more possibilities for "card-showing" doubles. I refer to the following as "card-showing" rather than responsive since on these you will usually have auctions where only one opponent has bid the suit at the time that partner doubles. These doubles are indicated on the convention card by writing "special doubles" under the section on negative and responsive doubles. The specific names are positional doubles, maximum overcall doubles, game-try doubles, and third suit doubles. Here is a brief analysis of each.

Positional doubles can be illustrated by looking at the following auctions.

Opener		Responder	
1 ♣	Pass	1 ♡	1 ♠
Dbl			

1 ♣	Pass	1 ♡	1 ♠
Pass	Pass	Dbl	

In the first case, opener is positioned behind the spade bidder, and a holding of A-Q-9-7 in spades would look useful on defense since it should be worth 3 or 4 tricks. Of course, if the partnership uses support doubles, those take priority for opener. In the second case, it is less likely that the heart bidder would want to make a penalty double, since his potent trump holding would be less valuable because it would be in front, or "under" the spade bidder.

Responder might have a hand like

♠ 8 5   ♡ A 8 6 4 3   ◇ K 7 3   ♣ K J 4

where he wishes to compete but has no convenient bid. The under-over principle is also usually applied to doubles by the 1 NT bidder, where

1 NT	Pass	Pass	2 ♡
Dbl			

is for penalties, but

1 NT	2 ♡	Pass	Pass
Dbl			

is takeout.

Both maximum overcall doubles and game-try doubles are based on the premise that in competitive auctions such as

1 ♡	Pass	2 ♡	3 ♣,

3 ♡ by opener is competitive and non-invitational. Therefore 3 ◇ is a game try, inviting a bid of 4 ♡ by responder but not necessarily promising diamonds. An insoluble problem arises when the opponents deprive you of a game try bid by bidding the suit directly below your trump suit. There is no game try bid available for opener on auctions like

1 ♡	Pass	2 ♡	3 ◇

or

1 ♠	2 ♡	2 ♠	3 ♡

so double is used here to invite game, not to try for penalties. Partner can jump to game, sign off at 3 of the trump suit, or if loaded in their suit, convert the double to penalties by passing.

So-called third suit doubles are used on auctions like

1 ♡	1 ♠	2 ♣	Dbl

It is illogical for the fourth player to double 2 ♣ for penalties since it is a forcing bid and usually shows 10 + points. With that hand you would prefer to pass and hope they get into trouble. Instead, the double shows length in the fourth suit (diamonds here) with tolerance for partner's suit. It would be a good way of competing with a hand like

♠ K 7   ♡ A 5 3 2   ◇ K 8 6 5 3   ♣ 9 4

Question: **You stated that you played that all doubles are responsive (takeout) after the opponents bid and raise a suit to the two level when they have opened. Is that also true when your side opens?**

Answer: Yes, very much so. Here are some auctions and examples.

| 1. | 1 ♣ | 1 ◇ | 1 ♠ | 2 ◇ |
| | Pass | Pass | ? | |

| 2. | 1 ♣ | Dbl | 1 ♡ | 2 ♠ |
| | Dbl | | | |

3.

	1♣	1♡	Dbl	2♡
	Pass	Pass	Dbl	

One (1) I would double with

    ♠ A 7 4 3 2   ♡ K 9 5   ◇ J 5   ♣ Q 7 4 or

    ♠ K Q 10 6   ♡ A 7 5   ◇ 9 7 4   ♣ J 10 6.

On (2) I might have

    ♠ 6 4   ♡ A 6   ◇ A 8 5 4   ♣ A K 7 4 3 or even

    ♠ A 7   ♡ Q 9   ◇ A K J 5   ♣ K 9 7 4 3.

Clearly it is correct to think of their auction as suit agreement, with the combination of a takeout double and jump.

For (3), how about

    ♠ A Q 6 5   ♡ 9 2   ◇ J 8 6 4   ♣ K 7 4 or

    ♠ K 8 7 4   ♡ Q 5   ◇ K 8 6 4 3   ♣ K 7.

The responsive double here preserves all options.

♠ ————————————————————————— ♠

We Bid and Raise (And RHO Interferes)

Before going into the actual rules that will govern this situation, a few comments are in order. Although this topic occurred while we were working on overcalls, the rules that were developed here also do an efficient job of dealing with auctions where we raise an opening bid. Therefore, we are including both opening bids and overcalls.

If the opponents use a support double, our redoubles are governed by *revenge redoubles* rules. All other auctions involving our low level raises with opponents' interference will follow these rules. By the way, if RHO doesn't interfere, most would interpret these bids identically. Here they are:

a. 2 NT = Invitational, natural.

b. Double Penalties—but after 1♡−Pass−2♡−3◇−Dbl, the double is artificial as a *game try* or maximal overcall double, since we have no reason to make a game try.

c. Cuebid = Asks for stopper for 3 NT. If the opponents have bid two suits, cuebid is telling, promising a stopper in the suit bid.

d. 2 of a new suit (reverse) is natural and tends to show extra values. It is forcing for one round.

e. 3 of a new lower suit is natural and forcing for one round. It usually promises at least game invitational strength.

f. Redouble, if available, says it's our hand and sets up a forcing pass situation for us. It promises at least game invitational strength as well. The redoubler's distribution could be balanced, but might not be.

g. This rule concerns itself with two mundane calls: pass and 3 of the trump suit. Neither of these promises anything great, but it is important to determine which of these is more encouraging.

In order to do this, the key factor is to determine whether we were forced after the raise.

Simple raises to the two-level are not forcing. After

1.	1 ♡	Pass	2 ♡	2 ♠	
	?				or
2.	1 ♣	1 ♡	2 ♣	2 ◇	
	?				or
3.	1 ♣	Pass	2 ♣	Dbl	
	?				

the side that opened the bidding may very well decide not to compete further. When we are not forced to act, a bid shows more offense than a pass, even if we bid only three of the trump suit.

On the other hand, there are times when we are forced to compete further. Some examples of these would be:

1.	1 ◇	1 ♠	2 ♠	3 ♣
	?			
2.	1 ♠	2 ♣	Pass	2 ♠
	Dbl	?		
3.	1 ♡	Pass	3 ♣ *	3 ◇
	?			
4.	1 ♠	1 ◇	Pass	2 ♠
	Dbl	?		
5.	1 ◇	1 ♠	Dbl	3 ◇ *
	Dbl	?		

*3 ♠ = Bergen raise, 4 trumps, 7-10 pts.;
 3 ◇ = Mixed raise

Notice that the raises that force our side to bid again are all artificial, either a cuebid or some other bid in a suit other than the trump suit. When this is true, the key principle to follow is that of *fast arrival*.

Fast arrival states: When we agree on a trump suit and are in a forcing auction, bidding the trump suit at the level we are forced to shows the least forward going type of hand. This principle is adhered to by many players, especially experienced ones. For more on fast arrival, refer to page 16.

Negative Free Bids

Suppose you hold a hand like

♠8 6 3   ♡K Q J 10 7   ◇J 9 4   ♣9 3

and hear your partner open 1 ◇. If your RHO passes you will respond 1 ♡ and probably have an easy auction, since you intend to rebid 2 ♡ over 1 ♠, 1 NT or 2 ♣, despite holding only a five-card suit. But your opponent doesn't look like he's about to pass. As he readies himself to speak, are you aware of how much trouble certain actions will cause you, while others will be no problem at all!?

For instance, if he doubles, you can bid 1 ♡ which, while forcing, doesn't promise much strength. In fact, some would jump to 2 ♡ over a double, showing a weak hand with a good six-card (preferably) or longer suit.

However, if your RHO overcalls 2 ♣, life won't seem so rosy at all. You can hardly bid 2 ♡, which promises at least a fair hand in addition to being forcing. If you pass, you may find yourself defending 2 ♣ (with both 2 ♣ and 2 ♡ cold), since partner would hardly be expected to reopen with a hand like

♠9 4 2   ♡A 8 5   ◇K Q 8 5   ♣A 6 4.

A negative double is possible, hoping (dreaming) of a 2 ◇ response from partner, so you can bid a nonforcing 2 ♡; but if partner rebids 2 ♠ or 2 NT, or if the opponents raise to 3 ♣, you are really not prepared to introduce your hearts at the three level. Negative doubling on what is basically a one-suited hand rarely seems to work out.

The problems may be similar after a 1 ♠ overcall. You have a better chance of surviving a negative double as partner's simple rebids will be below 2 ♡ if the next opponent passes. But a 2 ♠ bid by either opponent will once again see you confronted with "The Lady or The Tiger" decision between bidding your hearts at the three level and finding partner with

♠K 7   ♡8   ◇A Q 8 5 3   ♣K 8 7 4 2

or leaving your hearts on the shelf and missing a partscore or even a game opposite

♠5 4   ♡A 6 3   ◇A Q 10 5   ♣A 6 4 2.

Interestingly enough, if you are faced with a 1 NT overcall, you needn't feel any pain at all. Since you would be expected to double with a good hand, you can now bid 2 ♡ which is both nonforcing and weak.

Experience has shown that the problem of having a suit worth bidding without the required overall strength occurs quite often when our side opens the bidding. This is especially true when the opponents overcall and/or jump overcall. If the suit is long and strong enough and the vulnerability is right, we can sometimes solve our problem with a weak jump response – such as bidding 3♣ after 1◇ – 1♠, holding

♠9   ♡10 7 4   ◇10 6 3   ♣K Q J 10 9 6.

In practice, however, one or more of the necessary conditions always seems to be missing, such as the opponent bidding 2♠ (not 1♠), even with the above "perfect" hand.

Are there any solutions to these problems? Well, some of us believe there are. We call them "negative free bids," meaning that we make "free bids" which are neither forcing nor very encouraging. They are "negative" rather than positive and forward going.

For those of you who have never heard of "negative free bids," they are hardly mysterious and unknown. We encountered one when we considered 1◇ - 1 NT - 2♡. 2♡ is an example of a "negative free bid" which is standard and played by "everyone."

Another example of a type of "negative free bid" (hereafter referred to as NFB), for those who don't treat a new suit as forcing after an overcall, can be found in an auction like 1◇ - 1♠ - Pass - 2♣. 2♣ promises a good suit as well as suggesting a misfit for spades without promising a good hand.

Even the common overcall could be regarded as a NFB. Some other examples of NFB's are more sophisticated. Those who play unusual vs. unusual and/or unusual vs. Michaels treat an auction like 1♠ - 2 NT - 3♡ as nonforcing. If responder wanted to force in hearts he would cuebid the appropriate minor.

Many "big club" pairs use NFB's after opponents' interference. They play that 1♣ - 1♠ - 2◇ would promise 5 to 8 high-card points for responder and be nonforcing. If responder had a better hand he would jump shift or negative double and then bid.

Other examples of common NFB's are 1 NT - 2◇ - 2♠ and 1♡ - Dbl - 2◇. In both of these it would be normal for opener to pass, not expecting too much from partner.

Now that we have laid the groundwork for Negative Free Bids (NFB) by showing that they are neither unheard of nor a radical concept, it's time to zero in on what they show and when they occur.

Negative Free Bids occur after our side opens the bidding and the *opponents overcall with a one-suited hand.* This may be a simple overcall, a jump overcall or a double jump overcall occurring at the one, two or three level. *If responder now bids a suit at the two or three level, the bid shows a five-card or longer suit and is nonforcing, though responder may have a reasonable hand.* Responder usually has 5 - 10 HCP, about the same as for a weak two bid. However – depending on vulnerability, level of bidding and length of one's suit – on rare occasions responder may have as few as 3 HCP or as many as 11.

Here are some sample NFB auctions.

	PARTNER	RHO	YOU
1.	1◇	1♠	2♡
2.	1♡	2♣	2♠
3.	1♠	3♣	3♡

	PARTNER	RHO	YOU	
4.	1♣	3♦	3♥	
5.	1♥	1♠	2♣	
6.	1♥	3♣	3♦	
7.	1♣	1♠	2♦	
8.	1♣	1♥	2♦	
9.	1♠	2♥	3♣	
10.	1♣	2♥	2♠	

According to our definition, however, none of the following would be NFB's.

	PARTNER	RHO	YOU	
11.	1♦	1♥	1♠	(1-level)
12.	1♠	3♥	4♣	(4-level)
13.	1♣	2♣*	2♦	

*Opponents bid a two-suiter. (However, many experts play 2♦ as nonforcing in this sequence, just like an NFB.)

With both sides vulnerable, decide whether these are appropriate NFB's after 1♠ - 2♣.

a. ♠ A 5
   ♡ K 10 9 6 4 3
   ◊ 9 5 2
   ♣ 7 4

b. ♠ Q 4 2
   ♡ 9 8
   ◊ K Q 10 7 4 3
   ♣ 8 4

c. ♠ A 6
   ♡ K 4 3
   ◊ A Q 10 7 4
   ♣ 9 5 3

d. ♠ 8
   ♡ Q 7 4
   ◊ K 8 6 5 3
   ♣ 7 4 3 2

(Answers on page 60.)

Too Strong for NFB

What happens when we are too strong for an NFB, as in c above? We must negative double and then bid our suit. *This auction is game forcing and promises opening bid strength.* The following are examples of game-forcing auctions generated by East in an NFB partnership.

	WEST	NORTH	EAST	SOUTH
1.	1♡	1♠	Dbl	Pass
	2♣	Pass	2◊	
2.	1♠	3♣	Dbl	Pass
	3◊	Pass	3♡	
3.	1♡	2♣	Dbl	3♣
	Pass	Pass	3◊	
4.	1♣	2◊	Dbl	Pass
	2♠	Pass	3♡	
5.	1◊	1♠	Dbl	Pass
	2♣	Pass	2♡	
6.	1♠	2♡	Dbl	Pass
	2♠	Pass	3♣	

The only way to show

$$\spadesuit A\,6 \qquad \heartsuit K\,4\,3 \qquad \diamondsuit A\,Q\,10\,7\,4 \qquad \clubsuit 9\,4\,3$$

after $1\heartsuit$ - $2\clubsuit$ is to negative double, *then* bid diamonds. Opener must be prepared for the possibility that responder does not have four spades. However, this occurs only when responder has a game-forcing hand. Opener must still bid normally when responder makes a negative double, but should be sensitive to the possibility that partner has a game-forcing positive free bid. Therefore after

WEST	NORTH	EAST	SOUTH
1♡	2♣	Dbl	Pass
2♠	Pass	3◊	Pass

You hold, as West

$$\spadesuit A\,Q\,J\,6 \qquad \heartsuit K\,Q\,J\,6\,4 \qquad \diamondsuit 8 \qquad \clubsuit 10\,9\,4$$

and the one thing you must not do is bid 4♠. Just rebid 3♡ and await developments.

Opener's Alerting Responsibilities

When the partnership is using NFB's, there are a few considerations opener must remember. When a negative double is Alerted and an opponent asks for an explanation, reply, "Responder has a normal negative double with the unbid major (s) OR has a game-forcing hand (with an unbid suit) which may not look at all like a *normal* negative double." If responder follows up the double with a suit bid, this is also Alertable since it is forcing whereas most negative doublers would have a weakish hand.

Of course, when responder makes an NFB it is definitely Alertable. After $1\heartsuit$ - $2\clubsuit$ - $2\spadesuit$, opener should Alert and answer the opponents' question, "Natural but not forcing – usually 5 - 10 HCPs."

Opener's Responses to an NFB

When the auction goes 1♠ - 2♣ - 2♡ - Pass, opener may act as follows:

Pass – Minimum hand satisfied with hearts or has no place to go.

2♠, 3◊ – Lacking heart support, has a suit worth showing – non-forcing.

2 NT – Invitational to 3 NT with a lot of high cards – does not promise a heart fit.

3♡ – Preemptive raise promising support but not a lot of high cards. Responder will only carry on to game with the "right" hand.

3♣ – Cuebid. Game invitational raise.

3♠ – Natural, invitational, good suit, good hand.

3 NT – Natural, nonforcing, no heart fit.

4♣, 4◊ – Splinter bids in support of hearts – slam try.

4♡ – Natural – nonforcing, of course.

Imagine you are opener with the following hands after 1♠ - 2♣ - 2♡ - Pass. With neither side vulnerable, what do you do with each of the following?

e. ♠ A K J 8 4   f. ♠ A Q 10 6 5   g. ♠ K Q 7 4 3
   ♡ A 6   ♡ 9   ♡ K J 6 5
   ◊ J 10 3   ◊ A K Q 6 5   ◊ K 3
   ♣ 8 5 3   ♣ 4 3   ♣ 9 2

h. ♠ A K J 6 3   i. ♠ K Q J 10 6
   ♡ 8 6 4   ♡ 8
   ◊ A K 2   ◊ A J 3
   ♣ 9 5   ♣ A Q 9 7

(Answers on page 60.)

Next we will conclude our study of NFB's and see how their use enables us to free other auctions — like 1 ♡ - 1 ♠ - 3 ♣ - for some interesting artificial raises.

So far we have suggested that after a start like 1 ◊ - 1 ♠, a bid of a new suit (2 ♣ or 2 ♡) by responder can be used more efficiently when treated as nonforcing. This caters nicely to hands like

♠ K 6   ♠ 8 4 3   ♠ 9 7 4
♡ Q 9 8 4 3 2   ♡ 9 2   ♡ 10 6 3
◊ Q 5   ◊ 6 5 3   ◊ K
♣ 6 4 2   ♣ A K J 10 6   ♣ A J 8 7 6 2

which occur with reasonable frequency yet pose a nasty problem for Standard methods. Now it is time to consider the meaning of other actions that responder might take, starting with jumps in a new suit such as 1 ◊ - 1 ♠ - 3 ♣ /3 ♡.

What do 3 ♣ and 3 ♡ mean using Standard methods after 1 ♡ - 1 ♠? Most good players would play these jump shifts as preemptive in competition, showing something like

♠ 6 4   ♡ 8   ◊ J 7 3   ♣ K J 10 8 7 4 2.

Since *we* would make an NFB of 2 ♣ with that hand, jumps *below* opener's suit may be used to show something that might be more important. The hand type that may occur is a hand like:

♠ 9 4   ♡ A 6   ◊ Q J 9 7 4   ♣ J 8 6 4,

where we wish to compete to the three level while preempting the opponents by getting there as soon as possible, but are too good for a preemptive raise to 3 ◊ such as

♠ 8 4 3   ♡ 9   ◊ Q J 10 9 4   ♣ 8 7 4 3

or not good enough for a limit raise holding

♠ 9 7 4   ♡ A   ◊ K Q 8 6 4   ♣ 9 4 3 2.

The phrase we used to designate this type of hand is *the mixed raise*.

Not only has our use of 1 ◊ - 1 ♠ - 3 ♣ as a mixed raise worked out well when it has occurred, but we have profited from its nonuse when we've made other raises based on negative inferences. When we bid 1 ◊ - 1 ♡ /1 ♠ - 3 ◊, which we play as preemptive, we know that the upper limit for that bid cannot be too good since partner had a mixed raise available. Also when the bidding starts 1◇ - 1♡/1♠ - 2◇ we can be sure that responder has only four trumps, since with five he has both a preemptive jump and a mixed raise available at the three level – with the choice between those a function of his high cards.

Notice that after a major suit opening there are sometimes two new-suit jumps available at the three level – specifically after the auctions 1♠ - 2♣ - (3◇, 3♡ available and 1♡ - 1♠ - (3♣, 3◇ available). We designate the cheapest jump as our mixed raise, while using the second jump to show a limit raise in support of opener's major. Cuebids promising a limit raise or better are Standard today, but it must be better to avoid ambiguity when possible. By doing so, after 1♡ - 1♠ (overcall)

2♡	single raise with three trumps
2♠	game forcing raise
3♣	mixed raise (single raise with four or more trumps)
3◇	limit raise
3♡	preemptive raise

As we have often stated, we cannot have too many ways to raise partner.

How about a jump to the three level above opener's suit? We have found it best to play this as invitational holding a six-card suit. After 1◇ - 1♠, bidding 2♡ (nonforcing) on

♠8 3   ♡K Q 10 6 5 4   ◇K 6   ♣K 5 4

is somewhat dangerous, since it is at least two kings better than it might be. So we bid 3♡ on this hand, and whatever opener does should be just fine.

So, to summarize our jumps to the three level in a new suit, jumps below opener's suit are artificial raises while jumps to three above opener's suit are natural and invitational.

Are these the only sensible ways to designate these auctions? Of course not. One could play all the jumps as natural with any of the following strengths:

1) Preemptive, very weak.
2) Game invitational.
3) Game forcing, so negative doubles never need be bid on a one-suiter.
4) Slam tries, based on light jump shifts such as

♠A 10 4   ♡8   ◇8 7 4   ♣A K Q 10 7 4

after 1◇ - 1♠.

Imaginative readers will no doubt come up with other possibilities as well.

How about jumps to the four level? Take, for example, either single jumps such as 1♠ - 3♣ - 4◇, or double jumps like 1♡ - 1♠ - 4♣. Our concept is that all jumps to four of a major are natural and competitive (not strong), but jumps to four of a minor after a major suit opening are splinter raises. Obviously, other ideas are quite playable also, but it is worth noting that agreements are just as necessary for partnerships that do not use NFBs.

Do NFBs apply when made by passed hands? The best answer would be *no* and *yes!* No, in the sense that everyone treats the new suit as nonforcing by a passed hand, but yes in the sense that our free bids are lighter than Standard, and opener's rebids are defined in exactly the same way as the answers to an unpassed hand's response. We would bid 2♡ after Pass - Pass - 1◊ - 1♠, with

♠K 5 4 3   ♡Q J 10 9 6   ◊8 7   ♣9 4

Standard bidders would need more.

Our philosophy that a passed hand cannot have a suit worth jumping or bidding at the three level also enters into these auctions, so we would play that Pass - Pass - 1◊ - 1♠ - 3♡ or Pass - Pass - 1◊ - 2♣ - 3♡ does not promise hearts only, but is a fit bid promising hearts and diamonds with something like

♠8   ♡K Q 7 4 3   ◊A 9 6 5 2   ♣6 4.

One last thought. We have stated that opener should cuebid with a game invitational raise of partner's NFB, such as 1♠ - 2♣ - 2♡ - Pass - 3♣. What happens, however, when fourth hand acts so there is no low level cuebid available, for example: 1♠ - 2♣ - 2♡ - 3♣ or 1♠ - 2♣ - 2♡ - 3◊? The solution is for opener (when he has no convenient cuebid available) to double as a game try in partner's suit.

So much for negative free bids. Although we have put much effort and study into these methods, it remains an area that is still basically unexplored. Although many will decide that they do not wish to get involved with a radical departure from tradition, other more sophisticated readers may choose to give it a try. I look forward to hearing from them, secure in the knowledge that an exchange of ideas is the key to promoting the state of the art, particularly in the area of bridge bidding – circa 1986.

Answers to Negative Free Bid Quiz

a. Yes, an NFB of 2♡ is perfect here.
b. No, we must support opener's major. With one fewer spade, this would be a model NFB of 2◊.
c. No, we are too strong for a nonforcing 2◊ bid on this game-going hand.
d. No, the diamonds are too weak, the hand is lousy and we hate opener's suit.
e. Pass. Game is very unlikely, and hearts should be as good as anything else.
f. 3◊. The hands may be a bad misfit, but you can hardly suppress these diamonds. A new suit at the three level promises quite a good hand.
g. 3♡. Do not pass because you have a minimum opener. Never withhold primary trump support from your partner. Partner should Alert your 3♡ bid as preemptive and will usually pass, but if partner happens to hold

♠9 5   ♡A 10 9 7 4 3 2   ◊Q 6 4   ♣8

and bids 4♡, that suits you.

60

h. 3♣. It would be wrong to bid 4♡ and bury partner who might hold something like

♠Q 4   ♡Q J 10 9 7 5   ◇6 3   ♣8 6 4.

We want partner to bid 2♡ on hands like that. A game invitation with your hand is sufficient.

i. 2 NT. Natural, invitational, and a warning against hearts.

Bidding Over the Opponent's Takeout Double

After an opening bid and a takeout double, what strategy and style do you and your partner employ? Do you redouble with all 10+ point hands? Is a new suit a non-forcing rescue? Do you ignore the double and treat new suits as forcing, responding as in a non-competitive auction? Are jump shifts good hands? Are jump shifts preemptive? Do you use any conventions such as Jordan?

Before taking a look at modern tendencies, it seems relevant to examine traditional style. Standard practice was to treat *all* new suit responses as non-forcing, which meant that responder had a good suit but a weak hand. After 1♣ – Dbl, 1♡ would be bid on

a.   ♠ 6 5 3   ♡ K J 10 9 7   ◇ 8 5   ♣ 9 4 2

or

b.   ♠ 9   ♡ A Q 7 4 3   ◇ 9 5 4 2   ♣ J 8 3

but not on

c.   ♠ 8   ♡ K 9 5 4 3   ◇ A Q J 7 4   ♣ J 5
                        (too good a hand)

or

d.   ♠ A 7 4 3   ♡ K 10 5 4   ◇ 9 5 4   ♣ 8 6
                        (too weak a suit)

All 10+ point hands redoubled, regardless of distribution. Jump shifts were invitational, showing good suits and respectable hands. After 1 ◇ – Dbl, the call would be redouble with:

e.   ♠ A K 7 4 3   ♡ 9   ◇ K 10 6 5 3   ♣ 8 5

or

f.   ♠ A J 9 7 4 3   ♡ 9   ◇ 8   ♣ A Q 6 5 4

A jump to 2♠ would be made on

g.   ♠ K Q J 10 7 3   ♡ K 8   ◊ 6 4   ♣ 9 5 2

or

h.   ♠ A K J 10 8 3   ♡ 9 4 3   ◊ 8 6 4   ♣ 10

The above scheme probably doesn't strike you as being very efficient. Many others have arrived at the same conclusion. The following changes took place: new suits were forcing at the 1-level; jump shifts were preemptive; 2 NT was bid on good supporting hands.

These changes represented an overall improvement in bidding efficiency. After 1♣ – Dbl, we could sensibly respond 1♡ on

i.   ♠ K Q 6 5   ♡ 10 7 4 3 2   ◊ A 6   ♣ 6 4

2♠ on

j.   ♠ K J 10 9 8 5   ♡ 8   ◊ 8 4 2   ♣ Q 7 3

and 2 NT (the Jordan convention, invented by Alan Truscott) on

k.   ♠ A 6   ♡ J 4 3   ◊ 9 7 4   ♣ K Q J 6 5

Today these methods are standard among top players. Also, since Jordan is available to show a good hand with a fit, most now play that "Redouble Implies No Fit." However, "implies" is not the same as "guarantees," so a mild fit is possible. After 1♣ – Dbl, bid a Jordan 2 NT with "l."

l.   ♠ K J 6 4   ♡ A 8 7 4   ◊ Q 10 6   ♣ 9 5

but redouble intending to support spades later with "m."

m.   ♠ J 5 2   ♡ A 8 4 3   ◊ 6 5   ♣ K Q 7 3

Have any methods survived from the old style?

Most duplicate players still redouble on the majority of hands with 10 + points, including some top players. However, most good players are conscious of the importance of mentioning one's suit early in the auction. We concentrate on exploring for a fit as the first priority after 1♣ – Pass, and leave the point-count description till later. Why throw that out the window just because an opponent enters the auction?

It is recommended that you bid 1♠ after 1♣ – Dbl on

n.   ♠ A J 8 6 4   ♡ 9 3   ◊ Q 10 7 4 2   ♣ 8

or

o.   ♠ A Q 10 6 5   ♡ A 6   ◊ J 8 6 4 3   ♣ 9

In fact, some experts feel it is right to treat new suits as forcing at the two-level. After all, do you really think the best way to describe

p.   ♠ 9   ♡ A 6   ◊ A K 8 7 4 3   ♣ J 10 8 5

after 1♡ – Dbl is to start with a redouble?

Assume you are playing good modern methods: new suit forcing at 1-level; Jordan 2 NT; preemptive jump shifts. Neither side is vulnerable, and the auction has proceeded 1♣ – Dbl. What action do you choose with each of the following hands?

1.   ♠ Q J 9 5   ♡ A J 10 7   ◇ 8 4   ♣ 10 7 5
2.   ♠ 8 6 4 3   ♡ 9   ◇ 10 7 4   ♣ Q J 9 6 5
3.   ♠ K J 7   ♡ 9 6 4 3   ◇ Q 10 6   ♣ Q 9 4
4.   ♠ A Q 9 6 4   ♡ K 6   ◇ 8   ♣ J 10 9 7 4
5.   ♠ A K 7   ♡ 9 4   ◇ J 8 5   ♣ Q J 7 4 3
6.   ♠ A J 10 9 8 4   ♡ 6 4   ◇ 7 6 5 3   ♣ 8
7.   ♠ J 7 5 3   ♡ J 8 6 4 3   ◇ J 9 5 4   ♣ –
8.   ♠ A Q 6   ♡ 10 5 4   ◇ J 8 6 3   ♣ A 7 4

(1) 1♡. Just because an opponent makes a takeout double doesn't mean that your side can't play in one of the unbid suits.

(2) 3♣. This is preemptive showing good club support and that's all. With a hand this weak, don't worry about the four spades.

(3) 1 NT. You might have responded 1♡ with no interference, but 1 NT would be plausible even then. After the double, we shouldn't freely bid such a bad suit.

(4) 1♠. We want to bid spades and then strongly support clubs. When you have a lot to say, don't waste time with a redouble.

(5) 2 NT. This looks like a limit raise in clubs. Get the hand off your chest immediately.

(6) 2♠. Preemptive. Good suit, bad hand.

(7) Pass. Don't panic just because you don't want to play 1♣ doubled. The doubler's partner virtually never passes a low-level takeout double. Even if that happens this time, your partner should run after hearing of the big trump stack.

(8) Redouble. So you thought we would never redouble, did you? On this hand we are delighted to redouble. We have no suit to bid and nothing to mention distributionally, so it is nice to let partner know of our 10+ high card points.

Now we shall concentrate on auctions beginning with the double of a major.

Let's first consider a common situation. Partner opens 1♠ and is doubled, and neither side is vulnerable. Take a look at these hands, all of which contain spade support:

1.   ♠ K Q 4 3   ♡ 8 4 3   ◇ 10 7   ♣ 7 5 4 2
2.   ♠ A 8 4   ♡ 6 5   ◇ 9 7 4 3   ♣ J 5 4 2
3.   ♠ J 8 6 4 3   ♡ 9   ◇ 10 7 5 4 2   ♣ J 6
4.   ♠ A Q 8   ♡ Q J 3   ◇ 9 7 4   ♣ 10 8 7 3
5.   ♠ A J 8 3   ♡ K 5   ◇ 9 7 4 3   ♣ 8 4 2

6.   ♠ A 8 5   ♡ K J 4 3   ◇ Q 10 6 5   ♣ 9 3

7.   ♠ Q 10 6 5   ♡ 9 8 5   ◇ 9 7 4 3 2   ♣ 10

8.   ♠ 6 5 4   ♡ A J 6 5   ◇ 9 4   ♣ 8 7 5 4

9.   ♠ A 10 6 4   ♡ A J 3 2   ◇ J 7 5   ♣ 8 3

Let's look at the strongest ones, #'s 6 and 9, first. With each we wish to show a limit raise type of hand, so our thoughts run to Jordan. But primary trump support is required for Jordan 2 NT, which translates to at least four trumps. Therefore, bid 2 NT with hand 9, but redouble with #6, planning to support spades on the next round.

One treatment that has caused confusion is "Redouble Implies No Fit," particularly because it appears on the convention card under "over opp's takeout double." Because of Jordan, this is a viable idea, since we prefer to support immediately when possible. But since Jordan promises four trumps after a major opening, and since "implies" is not the same as "guarantees," it is normal for responder to redouble with good three-card support.

Of the remaining seven hands, one can be disposed of easily. #3 is an obvious 4 ♠ bid.

Some players would bid 2 ♠ on each of the other hands. The range for this is about 5 – 9 distributional points, with 3 + trumps. This is quite a wide range for a bid which occurs relatively often. #'s 1 and 7 have good offense but no defense, while 2 and 8 have a little of each. #'s 4 and 5 are almost worth redoubles, although even they are not all that similar in offensive and defensive potential.

Conclusion? It just can't be correct to bid 2 ♠ on all of them. Partner can't possibly judge what to do if he doesn't have a better idea of what you have.

More pressure should be put on the opponents on hands with good offense and little defense, such as hands 1 and 7. Therefore bid 3 ♠ preemptively on those two. This bid shows four trumps (occasionally five), with very little defense. In fact, some players reserve 3 ♠ for a hand containing nine points such as #5, but they represent the minority.

Are you nervous about getting up to the three level with weak hands holding four-card support? Don't be. Not only is it right to jump on hands like this, but even on hands like

♠ 10 9 7 3   ♡ 8 3   ◇ 10 9 7 4 3   ♣ 8 6

But how do you describe hands 2, 4, 5, and 8? Here's my suggestion:

Continue to bid 2 ♠ on hands like #'s 2 and 8. This shows three trumps and a minimum raise. Partner should continue only with very solid values.

With maximum single raises, I recommend using artificial raises. I call these B.R.O.M.A.D., which stands for Bergen Raises of Major After Double. When I first described this convention in April, 1981, my idea was to bid 2 ♣ with a good 3 trump raise like hand #4, and 2 ◇ with a hand like #5. However, since you should always be eager and willing to go to the three level with 9 + trumps, you should jump when holding the four trump raise. I now bid 3 ♣ with the mixed raise here, but some friends prefer 3 ◇ (in order to have a natural club bid available), while others prefer to jump to the suit 1-under (1 ♠ – Dbl – 3 ♡, 1 ♡ – Dbl – 3 ◇) in order to obtain maximum preemption.

For those who don't like giving up two natural bids, experience has shown that they don't come up too often. Also, when playing "BROMAD," opener knows a lot more about the hand each time he hears the weak competitive single raise (1 ♡ - Dbl - 2 ♡, 1 ♠ - Dbl - 2 ♠, which should be alerted as very weak, 5-7 distribution points, only 3 trumps) and these are the bids which will occur the most.

How do you play 1 Maj - Dbl - 3 NT? If it is undefined in your partnership, here are a few possibilities:

1. A balanced forcing raise with 4 + trumps, so that 2 NT guarantees exactly a limit raise. Some people refer to this as "extended Jordan." Or
2. A flat opening bid with 3 trumps and no doubleton offering a choice of games between 3 NT and four of the major.

Remember, as Ed Manfield wrote in *The Bridge World* some time ago, "We must have more ways to raise partner."

We have thoroughly examined responder's initial action after an opponent's takeout double. Next let's look at life from opener's point of view.

When responder has bid a suit, opener should make his normal rebid. Sometimes opener will be free to pass. This can occur in several situations:

- Responder raises opener's suit.
- Responder is a passed hand.
- Responder bids a new suit at the 2-level.
- Responder makes a weak jump shift.
- Doubler's partner bids something.

Try rebidding with the following hand in each auction presented:

♠ A Q 6   ♡ 8   ◇ K 10 8 7 4   ♣ A K 9 6

Assume neither side vulnerable for each.

1.   1 ◇   Dbl   1 ♡   1 ♠
                            ?

Bid 2 ♣. Although you have a misfit for partner's hearts, your extra strength allows you to compete for the partscore.

2.   1 ◇   Dbl   2 ◇   Pass
                            ?

Bid 3 ♣. Game is still possible if partner has a maximum. 3 ♣ shows your side suit as well as your promising hand.

3.   Pass   Pass   1 ◇   Dbl
                            2 ♡   Pass   ?

Pass. There are three good reasons for this call. First, the singleton heart cautions you to take it easy on this misfit. Second, partner's suit can't be too good as a passed hand since he didn't open a weak two-bid. Third, your strength is located in front of the takeout doubler, which suggests that your finesses are unlikely to succeed.

Now try doing the same thing with this weaker, balanced hand.

♠ A 10 9   ♡ K 10 9 5   ◇ 8 6   ♣ K Q 8 7

This time we'll assume that both sides are vulnerable.

4.		1♣	Dbl	1♠	2◊
	?				

Bid 2♠ in standard. You must support partner with three trumps in competition. In addition, the odds on partner's having a five-card suit are better than usual after his "free" bid. Of course if you're playing "support doubles" you would double to show a three-card raise.

5.		Pass	Pass	1♣	Dbl
		1♠	Pass	?	

Pass. You opened this hand in search of a partscore, and this looks as good as anything.

6.		1♣	Dbl	1♡	2♠
	?				

3♡. You would like to have a better hand, but your support is too good to suppress.

7.		1♣	Dbl	1◊	1 NT
	?				

Pass. You have nothing so say. (NOTE: Those who extend support doubles to minors would say the pass denies as many as three diamonds.)

Sometimes, though, opener will have to plan his rebid after partner has redoubled. This sets up a forcing auction, so opener is free to pass. In fact, since the opponents must run somewhere, usually the opener will not want to take the opponents off the hook. However, opener should clarify his hand if it is highly distributional, particularly with limited high cards.

Of course opener is encouraged to double the opponents with a good trump holding after partner's redouble. Actually, doubling out the opponents with the balance of power is the main goal of the redoubler, especially when you are playing against opponents who don't always wait for length in the unbid suits to make a takeout double.

What would you do with the following hands after 1♡ – Dbl – Redbl – 2♣? Assume neither side is vulnerable.

(1)   ♠ A Q 5   ♡ K J 6 5 4   ◊ J 7 3   ♣ K 5

Pass. If partner wants to double, that's fine with you. Failing that, he'll define his hand further.

(2)   ♠ K 6   ♡ K 10 8 7 4   ◊ A Q 9 7 3   ♣ 8

2◊. There will never be a better time to get your other suit in.

(3)   ♠ A 7 3   ♡ A 8 6 4 3   ◊ A   ♣ 10 7 4 2

Double. You have a great hand for defense, and you even know what to lead (◊ A). You might even catch partner with a stiff heart and have a defensive crossruff.

(4)   ♠ K Q 5 4   ♡ A Q 9 7 2   ◊ A 10 6 3   ♣ —

3 ♣. You aren't interested in defending against a low level club contract, and you have a great opportunity to show your three-suited hand with the club cuebid.

(5)　　　　　♠ K 7 4　　♡ A J 7 4 3 2　　◇ A Q 2　　♣ 6

Pass. You would rebid 2 ♡ with a minimum hand including six hearts. A pass followed by a heart rebid is used to indicate a better hand with six hearts.

That concludes our study of opener's rebids. However, there are a few other auctions to check out, such as responder's double jump into a new suit.

When your opponents are the redoublers, the takeout doubler's partner must concern himself with two responsibilities. Since his side may be in trouble, his first concern is to make sure his side finds a safe resting spot at a low level.

However, you should try to jam the auction with a good offensive hand. It's important to steal bidding room from opener's side – that's where the balance of power lies. Since three hands have shown strength, any jump by fourth hand should be considered preemptive.

Try these hands from fourth hand's point of view. Assume the bidding has gone 1 ◇ – Dbl – Redbl – ?, and the opponents are vulnerable. What call would you select?

(1)　　　　　♠ 9 4　　♡ 10 7 4 2　　◇ J 8 6 4 2　　♣ 9 5

1 ♡. Even with favorable vulnerability, you could be in real trouble. If you don't bid hearts, partner will never know hearts is the only suit you can stand.

(2)　　　　　♠ Q J 9 7 4　　♡ 8 5　　◇ Q 8 6 3　　♣ 4 2

2 ♠. You will be safe at the 2-level, since partner must have spade support and a respectable hand. You should bid 2 ♠ with this hand even if vulnerable.

(3)　　　　　♠ 9　　♡ 6 5 4　　◇ 8 7　　♣ J 10 8 7 5 4 2

4 ♣. Sock it to them. They must have a great fit in spades and/or diamonds. Let's see how well they'll bid starting at the 4-level. In fact, at this vulnerability some aggressive players might try 5 ♣!

(4)　　　　　♠ K 7　　♡ 9 6 4　　◇ J 7 5 4　　♣ J 7 5 4

Pass. It wouldn't surprise you to find that your best spot is in clubs, but what's the hurry? You can always get to 2 ♣ after passing, but if clubs is wrong, you'll be sorry you ventured to the 2-level when you might have survived at the 1-level.

(5)　　　　　♠ J 7　　♡ J 9 5 4 3　　◇ 8　　♣ 10 8 7 4 2

2 NT. Since you couldn't possibly have a good enough hand on this auction for a natural 2 NT, this must be unusual for the two lower unbid suits. Your opponents must have a huge diamond fit since your side probably has at least 17 cards in clubs and hearts, and both you and your partner are short in diamonds.

(6)   ♠ J 8 6 2   ♡ J 6 4 3   ◇ A 8 7   ♣ Q 4

Pass. You're not at all concerned about going for a number with this hand. In fact, you plan to compete for the partscore. The best procedure is to wait and see what partner bids, and then raise. Even if partner's longest suit is clubs, like with

♠ A 9 7   ♡ K Q 5 2   ◇ 9   ♣ K 8 7 5 2

it is clearly right for him to try 1♡ first, his cheaper suit.

Our last subject under the heading of "Bidding over the Opponents' Takeout Double" is to consider a few special auctions where a bid's meaning may not be so obvious. These auctions, definitely not for beginners, will take the partnership into the area of specific understandings.

1.	1♠	Dbl	4♣	
2.	1◇	Dbl	3♡	
3.	1♡	Dbl	3♠	
4.	1◇	Dbl	4♣	
5.	1◇	Dbl	4◇	
6.	1◇	Dbl	2 NT	
7.	1◇	Dbl	1♠	Pass
	2♣	Pass	2♡	

The first four all come under the general heading of double jumps into a new suit. #'s 1 and 3 begin with a major, 2 and 4 with a minor. There are three possible ways to treat each of these; splinter bids, natural preemptive bids, and fit-showing bids. Using the second auction as an example,

1◇   Dbl   3♡

Playing splinter bids, we might have:

♠ A Q 7   ♡ 9   ◇ K 9 4 3 2   ♣ K 10 7 5

Natural bidders might have:

♠ 8 3 2   ♡ K Q J 10 7 4 2   ◇ 6 5   ♣ 9

Those of us who use fit bids could have:

♠ 9 2   ♡ K 8 7 4 3   ◇ K Q 10 7 4   ♣ 8

promising enough to raise to 4◇ with hearts as well.

Which of these is preferable? Should you treat all four auctions the same? Or should you distinguish, say, the ones beginning with a major from the minor-suited ones? These are decisions that all experienced partners should make with each other. While these auctions will occur relatively infrequently, you might not enjoy the problem of guessing whether Partner has 1, 7, or some number in between in the suit in which he has jumped!

#5 is really quite simple. It is natural and preemptive, based on a hand with enough diamonds to risk the 4-level, such as

♠ 9 6 4   ♡ 8   ◇ A Q 9 7 4 3   ♣ 7 4 3

You might wonder why #6 is included when we have already decided to use it as a Jordan Limit Raise. But that means that

♠ K 7   ♡ K 6 4   ◇ K 8 7 4 2   ♣ A J 8

opposite

♠ 8 4   ♡ 9 5   ◇ A J 9 5 3   ♣ K Q 7 3

will bid to 3 NT via

1 ◇	Dbl	2 NT	Pass
3 NT			

Playing 3 NT from the side that exposes opener's major suit kings has to be wrong. Since it is preferable for opener to play 3 NT when and if we arrive there, some players invert the meaning of 1 ◇ – Dbl – 2 NT with 1 ◇ – Dbl – 3 ◇, so that 3 ◇ shows the limit raise. This is reasonable, since we would virtually never want to play 3 NT when responder has a preemptive raise. If you like the idea, it is referred to as "Switched Minor," and both responses become Alertable.

Auction #7 is mentioned since it means something very different in modern times. In the old "all good hands redouble" days, responder might have

♠ Q J 10 9 4   ♡ K J 10 9 6   ◇ 8   ♣ 9 3

or so, showing a weak two-suiter. But in today's enlightened "ignore the double" times, responder is bidding fourth suit forcing, showing a game-forcing hand and saying nothing about hearts, just as he would without the double. For this he might have

♠ K Q J 8 4   ♡ A 7 3 2   ◇ A 6 5   ♣ 9

not knowing what game he might want to play.

That concludes our examination of what should happen after an opponent's takeout double. The two most important concepts to keep in mind are: support with support and don't pass or redouble when you have something worth mentioning.

Question: **Can BROMAD be played after a minor suit opening?**
Answer: Absolutely. Larry Cohen and I play that after 1 ◇ – Dbl, all club bids from 2 through 5 show diamond support with more strength than the direct raise to that level. We also use 1 ♣ – Dbl – 2 ◇ as a "good" preemptive raise to 3 ♣. So after 1 ◇ – Dbl, we would bid 2 ◇ with

♠ K 9 3   ♡ 6 4   ◇ J 8 7 5   ♣ Q 9 4 3

and 3 ◇ with

♠ 10 9   ♡ 7 5   ◇ Q 9 8 7 5   ♣ Q 6 4 2

but 2 ♣ with

♠ K Q 5   ♡ 8 6   ◇ Q J 10 6   ♣ 9 7 4 3

and 3 ♣ with

♠ 6 5   ♡ 8 7 4   ◇ A K 10 6 4   ♣ J 7 3.

Question: **After a BROMAD raise, what do opener's actions mean?**
Answer: The principle of fast arrival is always the key. Any return to the trump suit by opener (even via a jump) is a signoff. Not only are

1♠	Dbl	2♣	2◇
2♠			

and

1♡	Dbl	2♣	Dbl
2♡			

weak actions, but since 1♠–Dbl–2♣ is really a form of raise just like 1♠–Dbl–2♠,

1♠	Dbl	2♣	Pass
3♠			

is a bar bid for us, just like

1♠	Dbl	2♠	Pass
3♠			

or

1♠	Dbl	2♠	3♣
3♠			

or

1♡	Pass	2♡	Pass
3♡.			

Unusual vs. Unusual
Unusual vs. Michaels

Conventional bids designed to show two-suited hands in competition are quite popular today with good reason – their frequency is comparatively high. Even my most inexperienced duplicate opponents all seem to use one or more of the following: Unusual Notrump, Michaels, Astro, Top and Bottom, Colorful, Hi-Lo, Roman Jump Overcalls, Upper Two, Copenhagen! And this is merely the list for dealing with natural one bids in a suit. Over big clubs we would include Truscott, Crash, Double for Majors, and Notrump for Minors. There are a lot more after a notrump opening, as well: Landy, Ripstra, Astro, Pinpoint Astro, Underside Two-Suiters. Even with all these, one must keep in mind that this is only a partial list.

Confrontations with these overcalls are inevitable, so our next step is clear-cut. It is not necessary to be familiar with the exact nature of each convention. We can ascertain which two suits are being shown at the table by way of the Alert procedure. However, it is necessary to know how to deal with them.

This brings up an important point about conventions which duplicate players would do well to remember. Although knowledge of conventions is helpful, one does not need to know all about those conventions which the partnership doesn't employ. However, it is crucial to have partnership understandings with respect to combating them.

With this in mind, we will engage in a detailed study of setting up defenses to the Unusual Notrump and the Michaels Cuebid – the two most often played of the two-suited bids after one-of-a-suit.

One of the reasons I advocate Michaels even with 5–4 hands is that my nonexpert opponents never seem to know what to do next. They haven't discussed whether 2♡ after 1♢–2♢ is a real heart suit, a raise in diamonds, or just a strong hand in general.

Please keep in mind that the defense I am going to present will handle any two-suited bid. Once the partnership masters this defense (or a similar one), they will be well prepared for any two-suited bid the opponents try. It is also worth noting that this is not the only defense to two-suited bids. However, I do believe (from my teaching experience) that it is the easiest to learn, and very efficient as well.

Let's begin with the Unusual Notrump. We will assume that a jump overcall in notrump by the opponents shows the two lower unbid suits (as virtually everyone uses it). This means that if we have opened a major, they are promising both minors.

The key principle to remember is that we always have two cuebids available, since we know their two suits. After 1♠–2 NT, 3♣ would be referred to as the cheaper cuebid, while 3♢ could be described as cuebid #2. OK. Here we go.

WEST	NORTH	EAST	SOUTH
	1♠	2 NT	?

3♣ (cheaper cuebid) = Limit raise or better (spades here).
3♢ (cuebid #2) = Game-forcing hand in fourth suit (hearts here)
3♡ = Natural, not forcing.
3♠ = Competitive raise (weak).

Notice that what we are doing is relatively simple. We are using the bid in their suit to give us a second, stronger way to show one of our suits. We will always follow the same concept in dealing with *known* two-suiters. Cheaper cuebid = good raise of partner's suit; Cuebid #2 = good hand in fourth suit. So after

WEST	NORTH	EAST	SOUTH
	1♣	2 NT	?
		(♡ & ♢)	

3♣ = Competitive (weak) raise of clubs.
3◇ = Good club raise (cheaper cuebid).
3♡ = Game-forcing spade hand (cuebid #2 = good hand in fourth suit).
3♠ = natural, not forcing.

Before going further in dealing with the opponents' Unusual Notrump, let's take a moment to give some examples and answer some questions. After

WEST	NORTH	EAST	SOUTH
	1♣	2 NT	?

South should bid 3♣ with

♠ A Q 8 4   ♡ K J 7 4   ◇ 9 2   ♣ 8 7 4 or

♠ A Q 6   ♡ 9 4 3 2   ◇ K 6   ♣ J 7 4 3 or

♠ A Q 9 5 3   ♡ A K   ◇ 8 5 4   ♣ 9 4 3.

South promises three or more trumps with either an invitation to game hand or a game force.

Bid 3 ◇ with

♠ A 4   ♡ K Q 10 7 4 2   ◇ A 6 3   ♣ 9 4 or

♠ A 2   ♡ A K J 7 4   ◇ 9 3   ♣ A 10 7 4 or

on almost any game-forcing hand with five or more hearts lacking good spade support.

3♡ would then be bid on something like

♠ 6   ♡ K Q J 10 7 4   ◇ Q 9 3   ♣ 8 4 2 or

♠ 8   ♡ A Q J 7 4 2   ◇ 9 4 3 2   ♣ 8 5 or

♠ J 6   ♡ Q J 10 9 7   ◇ A Q 6 5   ♣ 8 3.

3♠ rates to be the weakest bid of the four. The knowledge of a guaranteed fit can enable South to support partner with

♠ A Q 6   ♡ 9 4 2   ◇ Q 10 5 3   ♣ 8 7 5 or

♠ K J 7 4   ♡ K 6 5 3   ◇ 9 2   ♣ 8 7 5

or even

♠ Q J 10 6   ♡ 9 7 5 4 2   ◇ 8   ♣ 8 6 3.

Although I prefer to use cuebid #2 as a game force in the fourth suit, many prefer to use it with game invitational hands as well. There is no big advantage for one over the other – just make sure that your partnership is on the same wavelength.

What do bids beyond 3♠ mean after

WEST	NORTH	EAST	SOUTH
	1♣	2 NT	?

3 NT = natural, perhaps like

♠ 9 4 3   ♡ K 8 7 2   ◇ A Q 3   ♣ K Q 6

or even

♠ 8 4   ♡ K Q J 10 6   ◇ K Q 4   ♣ K J 5

– A hand that looks very notrumpy.

4♣/4◇ = Splinter raises of spades.
4♡ = Natural, maybe

♠ J 7   ♡ A Q J 10 7 4 3   ◇ 9 4 2   ♣ 8

4♠ is also preemptive, showing a weak hand which presumably would have bid 4♠ after 1♠–Pass.

♠ A 10 9 6 5   ♡ 8 7 4 3   ◇ 9 5 4   ♣ 8 or

♠ K J 6 4 3 2   ♡ 6 5   ◇ 4 3   ♣ J 9 5

would be reasonable.

Next we'll wrap up "Unusual vs. Unusual," including a look at which hands are suitable for doubles, and what double conveys to partner. We will get into "Unusual over Michaels," which is very similar to "Unusual over Unusual" but presents some new problems because there aren't always two *known* suits.

After partner opens 1♡ and RHO says 2 NT (Unusual), which hands are suitable for a double?

The answer, more or less, is the same hands that would have redoubled after 1♡–Dbl. South should double 2 NT with

♠ K 10 4   ♡ J 7   ◇ K 10 6 4   ♣ K J 4 3,

♠ A K 8 5   ♡ 10   ◇ J 9 4 3   ♣ Q 8 6 4,

♠ A Q 5 3   ♡ 8 7 5   ◇ K 9 3   ♣ Q 5 2 and

♠ J 9 5 2   ♡ K 6   ◇ A 7   ♣ Q 10 7 4 3.

The double of 2 NT shows 10 + high card points, indicating that the hand *belongs* to North-South. Forcing passes are therefore in effect – North–South cannot let their opponents buy the hand undoubled. They must either double or bid on to their own contract. The doubler usually lacks a fit with partner and has interest in doubling the opponents.

Meanwhile, what is opener's responsibility? Just as the double of 2 NT resembles the redouble of an opening bid, opener's assignment is also very similar. Opener can double the opponents with good trumps, make a descriptive bid with an offensive hand, or make a forcing pass. Let's see how this works. In each of the example hands, with neither side vulnerable, the auction begins:

WEST	NORTH	EAST	SOUTH
	1♠	2 NT	Dbl
3♣	?		

What should North do with these hands?

1.   ♠ A Q 10 6 5   ♡ K 5   ◇ 6 4 3   ♣ A J 7

Double. You have good clubs and good defense.

2.   ♠ A K J 7 3   ♡ Q J 8 6 4   ◇ 6 4   ♣ 3

Bid 3♡. With this good offensive hand, it is clear-cut to show your second suit.

3.   ♠ A J 6 4 3   ♡ Q 6 5   ◇ A J 5 4   ♣ 8

Pass. There is no other action to take.

4.   ♠ K Q J 10 7 4 3   ♡ A Q 4   ◇ 9   ♣ 5 3

Bid 4♠. No other action would be *bidding your hand*.

Now try the following hands where your side has opened the bidding in a minor suit. The fact that fourth hand passes doesn't detract from opener's responsibility to *bid out* a distributional hand.

Both sides are vulnerable.

			(You)
WEST	NORTH	EAST	SOUTH
			1♣
2 NT(◇/♡)	Dbl	Pass	?

1.   ♠ A 5 4   ♡ K 7 3   ◇ 8   ♣ K J 10 9 6 4

Bid 3♣. Although it is possible that partner has

        ♠ K J 7   ♡ J 10 6 5   ◇ A Q 6 5 4   ♣ 3

and the opponents have nowhere to go, letting your partner know about your club length is certainly the percentage action.

2.   ♠ 6 4   ♡ K 5   ◇ Q 7 3   ♣ A K Q 10 6 4

Bid 3 NT. This uncommon notrump bid should show long strong clubs with some red stoppers. It should be easier to make 3 NT than to "carry out" the opponents.

3.   ♠ A K Q 6   ♡ 9 4 3   ◇ 6   ♣ K Q J 10 6

Bid 3♠. Again you have a lot of offense, so let partner know. Not mentioning your spades could cause you to miss a good 4–4 or even a 5–4 fit.

4.   ♠ A 6   ♡ K 7 4 2   ◇ A 6   ♣ Q 8 5 4 3

Pass. Although you have more clubs than you promised earlier, that's no reason to rebid this moth-eaten suit. You have adequate defense with length in hearts, so sit back and see what develops.

Unusual vs. Michaels

If the opponents have announced which two suits they are showing, everything is the same as with the Unusual Notrump.

After 1♣–2♣ (majors), responder's bids follow the "Unusual vs. Unusual" pattern.

   2◇ = natural, non-forcing.
   2♡ = cheaper cuebid, limit raise or better in clubs.
   2♠ = cuebid #2, forcing diamond hand.
   2 NT = natural, invitational.
   3♣ = competitive club raise.
   3◇ = natural, great length, non-forcing.

3♡/3♠ = splinter raise of clubs.

3 NT = natural.

After a major-suit cuebid promising two specific suits, the structure is unchanged. If the opponents' cuebid promises the upper two unbid suits (as some play), then when the auction goes 1♡–2♡ (showing spades and diamonds) our bids show:

2♠ = cheaper cuebid, limit raise or better in hearts.

2 NT = natural.

3♣ = natural, non-forcing.

3◇ = cuebid #2, forcing club hand.

3♡ = competitive raise.

However, when the opponents use "ambiguous Michaels" after we open a major, promising the other major and an unspecified minor, we only have one cuebid available. We no longer can do it all. So when it goes 1♠–2♠ (hearts and a minor) our bids show:

2 NT = natural.

3♣ = clubs.

3◇ = diamonds.

3♡ = only cuebid, promises limit raise plus in spades.

3♠ = competitive.

We must decide whether the natural bids in a minor should show the game-forcing hand or the competitive strength hand. I suggest that 3♣ and 3◇ should be non-forcing, both because of frequency and the fact that they are impossible to handle otherwise. That means that we have to double with a hand like

$$♠ 6 4 \qquad ♡ A Q 4 \qquad ◇ 9 5 \qquad ♣ A K 10 6 4 2.$$

That is certainly not ideal, but fortunately this problem doesn't seem to occur very often.

One last point to keep in mind – when we do find ourselves defending against the opponents' two-suiters, it is usually right to lead trumps. Declarer rates to be short in dummy's second suit, so tend to lead a trump – even from a non-ideal holding.

We are now prepared for any two-suited overcalls the opponents may throw at us. Regardless of what two suits they show, they either specify the exact two suits or merely identify one of them initially. In either case, knowing what bids – especially cuebids – show must give us a better chance to survive the enemy attack.

Questions on Unusual vs. Unusual and Unusual vs. Michaels

Question: **If opener doubles the opponents after they select a suit after Michaels or Unusual NT, is that takeout or penalties?**

Answer: Basically takeout, although he could have a strong balanced hand. After

1♡	2 NT	Pass	3♣
?			

there is really no option for opener other than double with

        ♠ A K 7 3   ♡ A Q 10 6 3   ◇ K J 7   ♣ 8 or

        ♠ A K 6 4   ♡ A Q 10 7 4   ◇ A 6   ♣ 9 4

or even

        ♠ A K 6   ♡ A K 10 7 4   ◇ A 8   ♣ 9 6 5.

Lebensohl

How would you handle the following hands using Standard methods? Your partner has opened 1 NT (assume 15 to 17) and your RHO has overcalled a natural 2♠.

1)	♠ 8 6	♡ K J 10 6 5 4	◇ 10 6 4	♣ J 3
2)	♠ 6 4	♡ Q 8 7 5 3	◇ A Q 3 2	♣ K 5
3)	♠ 5 3	♡ A Q 9 7 4	◇ A K 8 6 5	♣ 4
4)	♠ 9 8	♡ A 6 5	◇ K J 7 4	♣ K 10 3 2
5)	♠ A 8 3	♡ A 6 5	◇ J 8 7 4	♣ Q 10 3
6)	♠ A 9 3	♡ K 10 7 4	◇ A 6	♣ 10 8 7 2
7)	♠ 8 6	♡ K 10 7 4	◇ A Q 5	♣ Q 9 8 4

With the first hand, we would like to bid a competitive 3♡, with no thoughts of game. On hands 2 and 3, though, we wish to bid a forcing 3♡, very possibly on our way to slam on hand 3. Since we obviously can't bid 3♡ weakly on some hands and strongly on others, we are left with an insoluble problem, regardless of how our partnership treats the 3♡ bid.

On hands 4 and 5, we are probably headed for 3 NT. However, if partner doesn't have a spade stopper, we wish to escape on hand 4. The standard answer is to bid 3 NT on each and hope, which once again leaves much to be desired.

It is easy to bid 3♠ on hands 6 and 7, as Stayman. If partner bids 4♡, we will have reached the correct contract. But what happens if partner doesn't have four hearts? He will then usually bid 3 NT. Now we are in the same position as on hands 4 and 5. If partner bids 3 NT without a stopper, we are going down on hand 7. If partner chickened out and didn't bid 3 NT without a stopper, we will probably be sorry on hand 6.

The point of all this is to illustrate the inadequacy of standard methods to handle the problems that arise when the opponents overcall a 1 NT opening bid. Because of this, a conventional solution, Lebensohl, was suggested a few years ago. The only natural bid that must be given up in order to play Lebehsohl is the competitive 2 NT bid, a valuable but not indispensable bid. In return, we gain the ability to easily handle any of the problems we encountered earlier, as well as a few others.

Here is how Lebehsohl works. After an auction like 1 NT-2♠ (overcall), a new suit at the three level is natural and forcing. If you merely wish to compete, responder bids 2 NT which forces opener to relay with 3♣. Responder now signs off by bidding his suit, or by passing if his suit is clubs.

On our first example hand, we would bid 2 NT, and over opener's 3♣, convert to 3♡ which opener will pass. On examples 2 and 3, we bid a forcing 3♡ and all is well.

We can also show partner whether or not we have a stopper enroute to game with or without Stayman. Here are possible sequences after opener's 1 NT has been overcalled with 2♠.

Opener	Opponent	Responder	Opponent
1 NT	2♠	2 NT	Pass
3♣	Pass	3 NT	
1 NT	2♠	2 NT	Pass
3♣	Pass	3♠	
1 NT	2♠	3 NT	
1 NT	2♠	3♠	

Just as we now have two ways of bidding a suit at the three level, we also have two methods of cuebidding or bidding 3 NT. The "slow" auctions (bidding 2 NT first) promise stoppers while the fast (cuebidding or jumping to 3 NT) deny stoppers.

With example 4, you bid 3 NT directly over 2♠, denying a stopper. If partner is also without stoppers, he will immediately retreat into safer waters. Holding example 5, you will bid 2 NT, then 3 NT which partner will pass even without a stopper since you are guaranteeing one. With example 6, you go through the 2 NT, 3♣ route to bid Stayman with a stopper, while in hand 7, the direct 3♣ bid will keep partner out of 3 NT if he doesn't have four hearts.

One problem we haven't been able to solve is the invitational hand, such as

♠ 6 4   ♡ K Q 10 5 3   ◇ K. 7 2   ♣ 10 8 4.

Using Standard over 2♠, we either have to underbid via 2 NT then 3♡, or overbid with a direct forcing 3♡. However, if the opponents overcall a natural 2♣ or 2♢, we can still invite. 2♡ is now the weak bid, while a jump to 3♡ shows the game-forcing hand. Therefore, we can use Lebensohl to show the invitational hand by bidding 2 NT and then showing our hearts.

What happens when your opponents make a two-suited overcall? It is still possible to play Lebensohl, and many do. Others play that since you have at least one two-level cuebid available, as well as double, Lebensohl is not necessary and 2 NT can be used as a natural bid. While either method is playable, for consistency it seems reasonable to play Lebensohl here also.

If we use Lebensohl in the above situation, we can then use cuebids to show the other two suits. Thus, after 1 NT-2♣ by the opponent (Landy showing the majors) – 2♡ shows a weak hand with clubs and diamonds and 2♠ shows a good minor two-suiter. Double would signify a hand interested in defending, usually one with length in at least one major. If only one suit is known, we have only one cuebid available, and then the cuebid shows support for all the unbid suits.

Because this can become quite confusing, let's clarify with some examples. Assume you are playing Lebensohl and the opponents overcall partner's 1 NT with a Landy 2♣. What would you do as responder with each of the following?

1)   ♠ K 6   ♡ 9   ◇ 10 8 7 5 4   ♣ Q 9 6 4 3

Bid 2♡. The cheaper cuebid shows a moderate hand with the unbid suits (minors). The hand should play well in partner's longer minor.

2)   ♠ 9 4   ♡ J 5   ◇ Q 6 4   ♣ Q J 10 8 7 4

Bid 2 NT. A direct 3♣ would be forcing, and double would show good defense. Partner will relay with 3♣ and we will then pass.

3)   ♠ 9 4 3   ♡ 10 6   ◇ K Q J 10 7 4   ♣ Q 5

Bid 2 NT. 2◇ would be weak and 3◇ strong. Therefore, 2 NT followed by 3◇ is invitational. We don't have this luxury in clubs since we have only two bids available, not three, so there is no way to invite in that suit.

4)   ♠ K 7   ♡ A 10 6 5   ◇ K 7 4   ♣ 10 9 7 4

Double. You will double 2♡ if the opponents land there, and maybe partner can double spades. There is always time to go to notrump later.

5)   ♠ K J 10 9 6 4   ♡ 8   ◇ 10 7 5   ♣ 9 3 2

Pass. You would like to play in a spade partscore, Landy or not. But 2♠ here is a cuebid, so you simply have to pass for now. After 2♡–Pass–Pass, you can back in with 2♠ if you are so inclined. I am.

We said earlier that the only problem with Lebensohl (assuming there is no memory lapse) is that you no longer have a natural 2 NT bid available. After 1 NT–2♡ overcall, we would like to bid a competitive 2 NT with each of these:

♠ K 7 4	♡ K 3	◇ 10 8 7 4	♣ Q 8 6 5
♠ J 7 4 2	♡ J 6 4	◇ A 8 5	♣ K 9 8
♠ J 10 7	♡ Q 5	◇ Q 7 4 3 2	♣ K 5 3.

However, there is an answer for these hands also. Over a one-suited overcall you can use the negative double. That will allow your side to compete for the partscore, and will even result in a penalty when opener is loaded in the overcaller's suit.

We can see how useful Lebensohl can be on these 1 NT auctions, and it has certainly accomplished what its inventors intended.

Lebensohl After 1 NT Questions

Question: **While playing Lebensohl after 1 NT, the auction went 1 NT–2♣–?. I wanted to bid a competitive 2 NT, but couldn't since that would force partner to bid 3♣. Should I give up Lebensohl?**

Answer: The above situation is certainly a troublesome one for devotees of Lebensohl. With a scattered 7–8 points you hate to sell out, particularly at matchpoints. Making a penalty double with something like two small trumps is insulting to the opponents, and it's not likely to be successful either. If you are willing to be practical, there is a pretty fair solution available. Use negative doubles! These will occur more frequently than penalty doubles, and you still have the option of "getting them" since opener could have a stack in their suit. Although not played by many, this device gains adherents each year.

Question: **Most Lebensohl adherents seem to use the "slow" auctions (bidding 2 NT first) to show the good hands with stoppers when followed by strong action. Is there any theoretical advantage to this, or could you just as easily play that "slow" auctions deny stoppers?**

Answer: Since the only problem in delivering our Lebensohl message is enemy interference, we get our fast (direct cuebid, direct jump to 3 NT) message in when lacking a stopper because they are less likely to be able to jam us when we have strength and/or length in their suit. But since this is only a minor advantage, if your partnership remembers "fast shows," go with that.

Question: **If we run from 3 NT because we have no stopper, must we go to game, or can we stop in four of a minor?**

Answer: Since two balanced hands with 24–27 high card points are unlikely to make eleven tricks, the logical answer must be that it is sensible to stop at the four level. After all, the non-Lebensohl players will be in 3 NT going down.

Question: **If we use the same methods after NT overcalls that we do after 1 NT openings (Stayman, transfers, etc.), should we also use Lebensohl in both situations?**

Answer: Yes, it should be identical.

| 1 ♠ | 1 NT | 2 ♠ | 2 NT |

should mean the same as

| 1 NT | 2 ♠ | 2 NT. |

My understanding with Larry Cohen is that we "IGNORE" their opening bid and "ASSUME" that the auction began with our 1 NT bid. Therefore

| 1 ♣ | 1 NT | 2 ◊ | 2 NT |

is identical to

| 1 NT | 2 ◊ | 2 NT, |

| 1 ♡ | 1 NT | 2 ◊ | 3 ♣ |

equals

| 1 NT | 2 ◊ | 3 ♣, | etc., etc.

Question: **What is transfer Lebensohl?**

Answer: Although not too many players use this, it has a lot of theoretical merit. After 1 NT – (opp.)2♠, 2 NT transfers to 3♣, 3♣ to 3◊, 3◊ to 3♡. The opening bidder becomes the declarer, which is clearly advantageous, and nothing at all is lost. I assume that there will be a steady increase in adherents to this concept.

Question: **I play Lebensohl as you wrote about it, but didn't know what to do with the following. I held**

$$♠ 6 4 \qquad ♡ 8 3 \qquad ◊ K Q J 8 6 4 \qquad ♣ Q 9 5,$$

and partner's 1 NT opening (15–17) was overcalled with 2♡. Should I have signed off in 3◊ (via 2 NT) or forced with 3◊, or gambled out 3 NT?

Answer: I sympathize with your problem, since you wished to invite but had no way to do it. I know of a group of players who use the direct bid (3◊ here) as invitational and give up on the forcing one, arguing that it is less likely to occur than the invitation. This seems very sensible based on the practical principle that game possibilities should always be higher in priority than those of slam.

Question: **I held**

$$♠ K Q 6 3 \qquad ♡ 9 4 \qquad ◊ Q 6 5 4 \qquad ♣ A 7 4$$

after the opponents made a natural 2♣ overcall of partner's opening 1 NT. I wanted to bid "Stayman with a stopper," which we do by 2 NT then a cuebid. But I couldn't cuebid 3♣ after partner bid that over 2 NT.

Answer: It's hard to imagine the club suit causing trouble when we can overcome interference in any other suit easily here. But that's the way it is, so all you can do is bid a direct 3♣ as Stayman, without promising or denying a stopper.

♠ ——————————————————————————— ♠

Lebensohl After Weak Two-Bids

Consider this all too familiar problem. LHO opens a weak two-bid in spades and partner doubles. You would bid 3◊ with

$$♠ 10 7 6 \qquad ♡ 9 2 \qquad ◊ 9 7 4 3 2 \qquad ♣ 10 6 4$$

and also with

$$♠ 6 4 3 \qquad ♡ A Q 7 \qquad ◊ 8 6 5 3 \qquad ♣ A J 4.$$

How in the world can partner ever judge what to do if our response can be anywhere from 0–11 points?

Once again, Lebensohl is the answer. By borrowing 2 NT, we now have two ways of bidding 3 ◊ – directly or by the slow route of first responding 2 NT. The direct route shows the better hand, although it is not forcing. Therefore, after an opponent's 2 ♠ – double by partner – and a pass, you bid 3 ◊ with about 7 to 11 points, and 2 NT followed by 3 ◊ with 0 to 6 points. There will still be some guesswork required for partner because we are starting at a relatively high level, but that's why the opponent opened 2 ♠.

When using Lebensohl after weak two-bids, the doubler's task is also simplified. Playing standard with

$$\spadesuit \text{ A Q} \qquad \heartsuit \text{ A Q 8 5} \qquad \diamond \text{ A 9 4} \qquad \clubsuit \text{ Q 8 7 3,}$$

we would prefer to double 2 ♠ in case partner has hearts, but if partner bids three of a minor we have to then close our eyes and bid 3 NT, hoping partner has something. Therefore, it is probably more practical in Standard to bid 2 NT. However, Lebensohl players can have their cake and eat it too. We will double 2 ♠, but if partner bids 2 NT, we will bid 3 ♣ and respect a signoff, knowing the values for game are not there. If partner bids his minor directly at the 3 - level, we can bid 3 NT with confidence, knowing partner has something.

Really though, the possibilities are endless as we are still on unexplored territory. You could play

2 ♠	Dbl	Pass	2 NT
Pass	3 ♣	Pass	4 ◊

as forcing since 2 ♠ – Dbl – Pass – 4 ◊ is invitational. Also

2 ♠	Dbl	Pass	2 NT
Pass	3 ♣	Pass	4 ♡

could be used as a slam try since 2 ♠ – Dbl – Pass – 4 ♡ shows a hand simply hoping to make 10 tricks.

Because of its great flexibility in doubling the number of sequences available to the partnership, Lebensohl is a convention destined to steadily gain in popularity.

Questions on Lebensohl after Weak Two-Bids

Question: **What should be the distinctions between the following auctions?**

A	2 ♡	Dbl	Pass	3 ♣
	2 ♡	Dbl	Pass	2 NT
	Pass	3 ♣	Pass	3 ♣
B	2 ♡	Dbl	Pass	3 ♡
	2 ♡	Dbl	Pass	2 NT
	Pass	3 ♣	Pass	3 ♡

C	2♡	Dbl	Pass	3NT
	2♡	Dbl	Pass	2 NT
	Pass	3♣	Pass	3 NT

Answer: You are certainly correct that there should be distinctions. That's what Lebensohl is all about. Since I don't believe that there is any standard answer for these (and I'm confident that many pairs have never discussed them), I'll tell you what we use here.

On **A**, we play both as invitational, but use the jump to promise 5 + spades, while the slower auction is based on only a 4 – card suit. This can be an important piece of information for the doubler when he has only three card support, which does happen.

For **B**, we designate the slower auction as a slam try, while the first auction is only seeking the best game, usually with four spades.

On **C**, the first auction shows uncertainty about whether 3 NT is the best contract, perhaps with

♠ 6 5   ♡ A 7 4   ◇ A 9 7 3 2   ♣ A J 5.

The slower auction promises more heart stoppers and therefore less doubt, perhaps

♠ J 5 4   ♡ K Q 10   ◇ K J 5   ♣ Q 10 7 4.

Question: **After**

	2♡	Dbl	Pass	2 NT
	Pass	?		

do I always have to rebid 3♣?

Answer: Although your partner may be intending to sign off in 3♣, there are several hand-types where it would be wrong to just say 3♣. Here are a few examples:

	2♡	Dbl	Pass	2 NT
	Pass	?		

♠ A Q 8 5	♡ 9	◇ K Q 8 6 4 3	♣ Q 5	Rebid 3 ◇
♠ A K Q 10 8	♡ 6 4	◇ A Q 5	♣ A 7 4	Rebid 3♠
♠ A K J 5	♡ 9	◇ A K Q 4	♣ A Q 6 5	Rebid 3♡
♠ A Q 10 6	♡ A Q	◇ K Q 10 6	♣ A Q 4	Rebid 3 NT

Fit Showing Bids

One of the most important concepts in bridge is the necessity to raise partner's suit, holding support. "Support with support," I continually tell my students. As we have observed, raising partner's suit is SO important that we are willing to invent artificial ways to show different kinds of support.

Auctions featuring Fit-Showing Bids have the following in common:

(1) One player has bid a suit – call it Suit "A"
(2) Partner bids another suit – Suit "B"
(3) Based on logic and partnership agreement, the second player's bid does not indicate a desire to play in Suit "B", but promises good support for Suit "A" with a reason for bidding Suit "B". Two good reasons for bidding Suit "B" are (a) to indicate length in the suit or (b) to indicate a good opening lead in case your side defends and partner is on lead.

When a suit has already been agreed, a Fit-Showing Bid may be made for the same reasons given above.

Obviously, Fit-Showing Bids are very handy on competitive hands. As one can never be sure which side will buy the contract, one must be prepared for the possibility of defending. Lead-directing bids can help your partner make the most effective lead for your side, bringing in many matchpoints and/or IMPs.

Fit Bids showing length will prove valuable in judging how high your side should compete. If partner shows club length along with heart support, you would not sell out to the opponents' 4♠ holding

♠ A 6   ♡ A Q 10 6 4   ◊ 3 2   ♣ K J 7 5,

but you would be happy to defend if your diamonds and clubs were reversed.

Although Fit Bids are most important on hands where both sides are bidding, they can also be helpful in constructive auctions. Holding

♠ A K J 6 4   ♡ Q 7 5 2   ◊ 8   ♣ Q 7 4

bid a game if partner shows an invitational spade hand with hearts, but decline the invitation if partner shows diamonds as a side suit.

We said earlier that Fit Bids are recognizable by logic and partnership agreement. Let's try some logic for starters.

1.
YOU	LHO	PARTNER	RHO
Pass	Pass	1♠	Pass
3♡			

Assuming that you play weak two-bids and that you know how to open one-bids and three-bids as well, will you agree that no passed hand could ever have a heart suit that one would pass, and then jump to three when partner opens 1♠? Will you also agree it's not a good idea to preempt your partner on a hand belonging to your side? *What 3♡ must show, therefore, is a hand with a spade fit and a side heart suit.* Your hand?

♠ Q 9 7 3   ♡ A K 10 6 4   ◇ 9 6   ♣ 8 5

would be about right. Notice what a good game contract is reached opposite the aforementioned

♠ A K J 6 4   ♡ Q 7 5 2   ◇ 8   ♣ Q 7 4.

Also notice that game would have no play if responder's hearts and diamonds were reversed. In that case responder would jump to 3◇ over 1♠ and opener would sign off in 3♠, aware of the wasted values.

2. You hold

♠ 8 6 3   ♡ A K J 9 7 4   ◇ —   ♣ K 6 5 4

RHO	YOU	LHO	PARTNER
1◇	1♡	1♠	2♡
3♠	?		

Isn't it clear to bid 4◇, to insure that you will get a diamond lead against the opponents' eventual 4♠ contract? Isn't it foolish to play 4◇ as a cuebid suggesting slam, as ostensibly it is? Also, won't partner be able to tell from his diamond length and dummy's opening bid that this is a lead-director, not a length-showing Fit Bid?

Even if you had never heard of a lead-directing Fit Bid, isn't this the only logical interpretation of 4◇ in this sequence? In fact, partner can even use suit-preference on the opening lead! What if the opponents choose not to bid 4♠? That would be surprising considering your hand and the auction. However, even if you are not able to take 10 tricks, the damage at 4♡ will be modest. And it *must* be right to get a diamond lead against 4♠ if they DO bid it.

3.

	PARTNER	RHO	YOU
	3◇	Dbl	4♣

Don't you think that any player smart enough to choose you for a partner would interpret your 4♣ bid correctly? Could you ever want to play in clubs at a higher level when your RHO showed a good hand with probably length in clubs and your partner said the hand should play in diamonds? No, of course not. This must be a diamond raise requesting a club lead, very useful since partner will probably be the opening leader after fourth hand responds to the takeout double. Perhaps you hold

♠ 8 5 2   ♡ 8 5 2   ◇ 9 4 3   ♣ A Q 10 6.

If your hand happened to be

♠ 8 5 2   ♡ 8 5 2   ◇ A Q 9   ♣ 10 9 5 3,

you would bid 4◇, presumably asking for a diamond lead as you didn't ask for another lead by bidding some other suit.

We have only scratched the surface on Fit-Showing Bids. The possibilities are almost endless. If you have been concerned about your partner's competitive judgment and opening leads of late, maybe he will stop giving you fits if you start showing your fits.

Lead-Directing Raises

Now we will look at fit-showing bids that are lead-directing. Getting partner off to the right lead is particularly important at matchpoints, but a good opening lead can be worth a lot of **IMPs** as well.

Say you hold

$$\spadesuit\ A\ Q\ 10\ 9\ 7\ 3 \qquad \heartsuit\ Q\ 5 \qquad \diamondsuit\ 8\ 7\ 3 \qquad \clubsuit\ 10\ 9$$

and the bidding goes

LHO	PARTNER	RHO	YOU
Pass	Pass	1 ◊	2 ♠
3 ◊	3 ♡		

Can partner seriously want to play 3 ♡ opposite a weak jump overcall when hearts weren't worth mentioning at the first turn? No! This must be a fit-showing bid.

Is it a *lead-director* or a *length-shower?*

There are two good reasons why it is a lead-director.

First, *you have made a preemptive bid.* Partner would never show length in a suit, expecting you to take further action, after a preempt. We show length in a suit only so that partner can make an intelligent final decision about where to play the hand. This does not apply when you have already shown your only suit in a weak hand.

Second, *the weak jump overcaller will be on lead* against diamonds (or notrump) if our side ends up defending. So you lead a heart and partner returns a spade. The 3 ♡ bidder's hand might look like

$$\spadesuit\ J\ 6\ 2 \qquad \heartsuit\ A\ K\ 10\ 6 \qquad \diamondsuit\ 5\ 4 \qquad \clubsuit\ 8\ 6\ 4\ 3.$$

With this hand your partner is willing to compete to 3 ♠, but is anxious to have you lead hearts against either a diamond or a notrump contract so he can lead spades for you.

Once this principle has been accepted, then many other auctions are clarified. Assume you hold

$$\spadesuit\ J\ 7\ 5\ 2 \qquad \heartsuit\ K\ Q\ 10\ 6\ 4 \qquad \diamondsuit\ 8 \qquad \clubsuit\ 9\ 5\ 3$$

and hear the following auction:

YOU	LHO	PARTNER	RHO
Pass	1 ◊	2 ♠	3 ♣

You are willing to compete to 4 ♠, but clearly want a heart lead if your side defends. Isn't it logical to bid 4 ♡, showing a raise to 4 ♠ but desiring a heart lead? How could this possibly be natural after your original pass?

What about this auction?

YOU	LHO	PARTNER	RHO
Pass	1♣	1♡	Dbl*
2♠			*Negative

After the opponent's negative double, what are the odds that you would have good enough spades to make a natural jump to 2♠? Even if that was barely possible, your passed hand status would rule that out. What 2♠ must mean, of course, is a raise to 3♡ with good spades. You might have some hand such as

♠ A Q 10 6   ♡ K 8 7 4   ◇ 9 3 2   ♣ 8 5

2♠ could also be played as a splinter bid. However, splinters are less valuable and occur less often than the lead-director fit-showing raises.

Here is another case.

YOU	LHO	PARTNER	RHO
Pass	1♠	2◇	2♠
3♡			

If you play weak two-bids, we can't assume that you neglected to open the bidding with 2♡. The 3♡ bidder should have diamond support with heart values – something like:

♠ 9 4   ♡ A K J   ◇ J 10 4 2   ♣ 8 6 4 2

Notice that lead-directing fit bids usually contain length as well – but don't necessarily have to.

Here's one more before we establish some rules and summarize.

YOU	LHO	PARTNER	RHO
Pass	1♡	2 NT	Dbl
3♠			

Isn't this clearly a lead-directing fit bid with a fit in one or both minors? Isn't that a more *helpful* way to bid

♠ A Q J 8   ♡ 8 6   ◇ 10 7 4 3 2   ♣ 8 7

than any number of diamonds? Won't partner be grateful to know that it's right for him to lead spades from

♠ K 6   ♡ 9   ◇ K J 9 6 5   ♣ K 10 6 4 3

against a heart contract? Do you think he would have found that lead on his own?

Time now for some rules.

Rules for passed hands opposite:

> *Simple Overcalls*
> *Two-Suited Bids*
> *Jump Overcalls*
> *Opening Preempts*

1. JUMPS into new suits are always fit bids.
2. Non-jump new suit bids are fit bids – with one exception. After a simple overcall by partner, a new suit bid is natural if made at the 1 - level or the 2 - level. Notice that this rule covers auctions like

YOU	LHO	PARTNER	RHO
Pass	1♣	1◊	Pass
1♠			
or			
Pass	1♠	2♣	Pass
2♡			

where you could easily want to show a five-card suit of your own, with or without a fit for partner's suit.
3. These fit bids are invariably lead-directing, usually with length in the suit as well.
4. A passed hand cannot show a long suit of his own on these auctions. Therefore, if as dealer you have a long suit worth showing, try hard to get it in on your first turn.

Are lead-directing fit bids Alertable? Although they are based on bridge logic, not everyone uses this treatment. Therefore you should Alert fit bids. After

PARTNER	RHO	YOU	LHO
Pass	1♠	2♡	2♠
3♣			

I would Alert and reply to a question, "3♣ is a heart raise requesting a club lead."

More Lead-Directing Raises

We began by confining our discussion of lead-directing raises to those made by passed hands, since those were more obvious and offered a logical place to begin. Now we are ready to seek out some less obvious lead-directors.

In our first discussion on fit-showing bids, we said that 3◊ – Dbl – 4♣ must be a diamond raise desiring a club lead rather than clubs. Since we *couldn't* have enough clubs to want to play clubs at the 4 - level, then we certainly *wouldn't* want to introduce clubs at the 5 - level after partner preempted 3◊; so 3◊ – Dbl – 5♣ is a diamond raise to the 5 - level desiring a club lead. How about a hand like

♠ 9   ♡ 8 6 4 3   ◊ Q 9 6 4   ♣ A Q 10 6?

With that in mind, what should 3◊ – Dbl – 4 NT show? If we agree that it must be a diamond raise of some kind, and that the lead-directing aspect is the most important information that one can give to the preempter, what lead can you be asking for? How about a hand like

♠ 9   ♡ A Q 10 6   ◊ Q 9 6 4   ♣ 8 6 4 3?

But then we could have bid 3 ♡ or 4 ♡ to get a heart lead. But don't we want to get past 4 ♠ – which must be a good spot for the opponents? Play 4 NT to show a raise to 5 ◊ desiring a major suit lead, and if the opponents bid 5 ♠, partner will have no trouble leading hearts.

Are these treatments for everyone? Of course not. But these situations do occur, and the principle is not unknown, though it could be applied more frequently.

What about 3 ◊ – Dbl – 5 ◊? That would normally be straightforward enough, but since we have the aforementioned ways to ask for other suits being led, shouldn't 5 ◊ ask for a diamond lead? How about this hand:

♠ 8 3   ♡ 9 4   ◊ A K 9 4   ♣ 10 7 6 4 3?

Could we go so far as to say that after an opponent's takeout or negative double after our preempt, a new suit is always a lead-director? We don't want to play in our own suit when partner has shown a one-suiter and the opponents hold the unbid suits.

Yes, this rule is a valid one, recommended as the best way to define these auctions. Therefore 2 ♠ – Dbl – 3 ♣ shows something like

♠ J 7 4   ♡ K 8 5   ◊ 8 4   ♣ K J 9 7 4.

Here are a few other auctions that are easily defined by our new rule. Sample hands are included as well.

	PARTNER		YOU
	2 ♡	Dbl	4 ♣

♠ 6 4   ♡ Q 10 7 5   ◊ 9 4 3   ♣ A K J 9

	PARTNER		YOU
1 ♣	2 ♡	Dbl	3 ◊

♠ 6 4 2   ♡ 10 7 4   ◊ A Q J 8 2   ♣ 5 3

	PARTNER		YOU
1 ◊	2 ♡	Dbl	3 ♠

♠ A Q 10 9   ♡ J 7 5 4 3   ◊ 9   ♣ 8 7 4

	PARTNER		YOU
1 ♡	2 ♠	Dbl	3 ♠

♠ K Q 6   ♡ A 5 4 2   ◊ 8 7 2   ♣ 8 6 4

	PARTNER		YOU
	4 ♡	Dbl	5 ♣

♠ –   ♡ J 10 5 2   ◊ J 6 4 3 2   ♣ K Q 10 8

We are still not finished with lead-directing fit-bids, not to mention the artificial and conventional fit-bids. Would you have doubts about the meaning of 1 ♡ – 4 ♣ – 4 ♡ – 4 ♠ if it came up while playing with a good, although non-regular partner? Isn't partner more likely to have a hand resembling

♠ A K 6 5   ♡ 9 3   ◊ 10 7 4 2   ♣ Q J 9

rather than

♠ A K Q 10 7 4 3 2   ♡ 8   ◊ K 7   ♣ 9 4?

Isn't a 4♠ bid after 1♡ – 2 NT – 4♡ quite unusual? What are the odds that someone holds an independent suit? But isn't 4♠ an excellent temporary bid on

♠ K Q 10   ♡ A   ♢ J 10 9 6 4   ♣ 8 7 5 2?

Of course, if the opponents double the fit-bid you can pass, catering to the unlikely possibility of a *very* long independent suit opposite.

There are still lots of auctions requiring thought and discussion. Remember, "support with support," but there's more than one way to tell partner you like his suit, especially if you prefer that partner frequently "find you" with accurate opening leads.

 ──

After a Fit is Found

Everyone is familiar with an auction like

1♠   Pass   2♠   Pass
3♢

Opener is trying for game (possibly even slam) and chooses to focus particular attention on diamonds. Even though there is virtually no chance that he wishes to play in diamonds. Depending on partnership agreement, 3♢ may be (1) a short-suit game try, promising at most a singleton diamond, (2) a long suit game try, promising diamond length, (3) a "need help" game try, showing 3 + weakish diamonds requiring strength or shortness from partner.

A partnership must agree on one of these and presumably most have, although the answer that I usually get when I ask about an auction like this is, "Duh, I don't know what it means."

If we do assume that the above auction has been discussed by good partnerships, there are many similar auctions where some of the best of regular partnerships may be on shaky ground. Try these out:

1.	1♠ 4♢	Pass	2♠	Pass
2.	1♠ 4♣	Pass	2♠	3♢
3.	1♠ 4♠	Pass	2♠	3♢
4.	1♠ 4♢	Pass	2♠	3♢
5.	1♠ 3♢	Pass	2♠	3♣

| 6. | 1♠ | Pass | 2♠ | 3♣ |
| | Dbl | | | |

| 7. | 1♠ | Pass | 2♠ | 3♡ |
| | Dbl | | | |

| 8. | 1♠ | Pass | 2♠ | 3♡ |
| | 3♠ | | | |

| 9. | 1♠ | Pass | 2♠ | 3◇ |
| | 3♡ | | | |

| 10. | 1♡ | 2♣ | 2♡ | 3♣ |
| | Dbl | | | |

| 11. | 1♡ | 2◇ | 2♡ | 3◇ |
| | Dbl | | | |

| 12. | 1♡ | 2♣ | 2♡ | 3♣ |
| | 3◇ | | | |

| 13. | 1♡ | Pass | 2♡ | Pass |
| | 3♡ | | | |

| 14. | 1♡ | Pass | 2♡ | 2♠ |
| | 4♣ | | | |

| 15. | 1♡ | 1♠ | 2♡ | 2♠ |
| | 3♠ | | | |

| 16. | 1♡ | 1♠ | 2♡ | 3♠ |
| | 4♣ | | | |

| 17. | 1◇ | 1♡ | 1♠ | 2♡ |
| | Pass | 3♡ | | |

| 18. | 1♣ | Pass | 1♡ | 1♠ |
| | 2♡ | Pass | 3♡ | |

Eventually I will discuss each of these 18 auctions in detail, including my suggestions where warranted. Keep in mind that my goal is not to convince readers to do things my way, but to show the necessity for partnership agreement.

| 1. | 1♠ | Pass | 2♠ | Pass |
| | 4◇ | | | |

Obviously this is a slam try, since opener could have bid 4♠. It must either show long diamonds like

♠ A J 8 7 4 3   ♡ A 8   ◇ A K 10 8 5   ♣ —

or short diamonds (splinter) like

♠ A Q 7 6 5 4   ♡ A Q 6   ◇ —   ♣ A J 7 2.

90

As you can see, both of these interpretations can be useful when the appropriate hand is held, suggesting slam if responder has the right hand. I suspect that it's correct to use 4 ◊ (as well as 4♣ and 4♡) to indicate a long suit slam try, but neither will occur too often.

2.   1♠   Pass   2♠   3◊
               4♣

We saw in the previous example how good a hand we need for a slam try; surely we don't rate to hold one of those too often. Therefore, when the opponents interfere, it is more practical to worry about doing the right thing competitively than to dream about slam. If the opponents compete to 5◊ , it is crucial for the partnership to know whether to double, pass, or compete to 5♠. Therefore, 4♣ here should show a very good hand with clubs, setting up a forcing auction if the opponents compete to 5◊. It could be the start of a slam exploration, but that is less likely. Partner can cuebid 4◊ or 4♡ with the right hand, but can never go past 4♠ on his own. If 4♣ suggests a hand like

♠ A J 8 5 4 3   ♡ A 7   ◊ 8   ♣ A K 9 4

then partner can compete to 5♠ on

♠ K Q 7 2   ♡ 9 6 4 2   ◊ 6 5   ♣ Q J 7,

and double with

♠ Q 7 2   ♡ K J 8 6   ◊ J 4 2   ♣ 8 6 5.

Of course, if the opponents sell out to 4♠, all the better.

3.   1♠   Pass   2♠   3◊
               4♠

How could there be a more straightforward auction than this? Why am I wasting time with this auction? The answer to this one can be found in the analysis of auction 2. If we always lazily jump to 4♠ with a good hand, how will anyone know what to do if and when the opponents continue on to 5◊? Are we forced to take further action over 5◊? Or might it be their hand and we had better get out while we can? Haven't you jumped to 4♠ over 3◊ on

♠ A K 9 7 4 3 2   ♡ K J 7   ◊ 8   ♣ 9 2

and

♠ A K J 8 7 3   ♡ A Q 7   ◊ 9 2   ♣ K 8

as well as the aforementioned

♠ A J 8 5 4 3   ♡ A 7   ◊ 8   ♣ A K 9 4?

If you are too good a partner to be so lazy, don't you know someone else who isn't so blameless?

What's the solution? Rather simple, actually. In a competitive auction, we must do better than just jump to 4♠ with all attractive hands. We are now ready to define auctions 2, 3, and 4 simultaneously. After

1♠	Pass	2♠	3◇

opener should bid 4♣ with a hand like

♠ A J 8 5 4 3   ♡ A 7   ◇ 8   ♣ A K 9 4,

setting up a forcing situation at the five level while showing a very good hand with a side club suit.

4♠ simply says I'm willing to play 4♠, but if the opponents continue to the five level, partner is on his own. He can pass, double, or bid 5♣, and whichever he chooses, I will not get in his way. Think of 4♠ as a preempt, and once you preempt, you are out of the picture.

♠ A K 9 7 4 3 2   ♡ K J 7   ◇ 8   ♣ 9 2

is certainly a hand which fits this mold.

4.   4◇ also serves to set up a forcing auction at the five level. This cuebid is not a slam try (although slam is possible) but states that this hand belongs to our side and we cannot let the opponents play undoubled. It shows a lot of high cards, but doesn't emphasize any second suit.

♠ A K J 8 7 3   ♡ A Q 7   ◇ 9 2   ♣ K 8

is the reasonable example we used earlier.

5.

	1♠	Pass	2♠	3♣
	3◇			

This must be a game try, inviting partner to jump to 4♠ with a suitable hand. Does it mean the same as this sequence?

	1♠	Pass	2♠	Pass
	3♡			

You could play it that way, but I think it is more important in competitive auctions to show your suits. Most play

	1♠	Pass	2♠	Pass
	3◇			

as a *need help* game try perhaps based on

♠ A J 10 6 4 3   ♡ 8   ◇ Q 7 5   ♣ K Q J.

However

	1♠	Pass	2♠	3♣
	3◇			

should show a diamond suit as well as a hand with at least some interest in game.

♠ A J 8 7 5   ♡ Q 6   ◇ A Q J 4 2   ♣ 8

seems about right.

6.

	1♠	Pass	2♠	3♣
	Dbl			

You could treat this as a penalty double since both opponents have not agreed on a suit and may be out on a limb. However, experience has suggested that the frequency of purely penalty doubles is relatively rare. Also if 3♦ and 3♡ here show suits, what do we do with a balanced game try, such as

♠ A J 10 6 4   ♡ A 8 7   ♦ A Q   ♣ J 7 4?

So double here should be *optional* suggesting a good fairly balanced hand. Responder can pass, sign off in 3♠ or jump to 4♠. In fact, responder can even make a return game try of 3♦ with a hand like

♠ K 9 5 2   ♡ 9 6 3   ♦ K J 10 9   ♣ 8 5

where he is not sure whether to bid 3♠ or 4♠.

7.		1♠	Pass	2♠	3♡
		Dbl			

This may appear to be the same type of auction as #6, but the relative rank of the suits puts this auction in a different perspective. Since 3♠ is clearly a competitive bid here, a double must be a game try – in fact, the only game try. Since we would double with

♠ A 10 8 7 5   ♡ 9   ♦ A Q 10 6   ♣ A 10 7

or with

♠ Q J 8 6 3   ♡ 9 2   ♦ A K Q 7 3   ♣ 8,

responder can leave in this double only with a heart stack of his own, like

♠ K 4 2   ♡ Q J 10 6   ♦ J 5   ♣ Q 6 5 3.

This double is referred to as a maximal overcall double, or a game try double. It is definitely Alertable, although most experts have been using it for a long time.

8.				
	1♠	Pass	2♠	3♡
	3♠			

We managed to define this auction in our discussion of Auction #7. 3♠ is a purely competitive bid, showing no interest in game, but a reason for competing to 3♠. It would be correct to refer to this as a bar bid.

♠ K Q J 5 4 3   ♡ 3 2   ♦ A 9 8 6   ♣ 9,

♠ A Q 10 7 4   ♡ 9   ♦ A Q 8 5   ♣ 9 4 3,

and

♠ A K Q J 7   ♡ 6   ♦ 8 5   ♣ J 7 6 5 4

all would be plausible hands for this sequence.

9.		1♠	Pass	2♠	3♦
		3♡			

Once again we have an auction which appears similar to an already discussed sequence (#5), but there are some subtle differences. After 3♣ we had room to show either a diamond suit or a heart suit, but 3◊ leaves room only for one in-between bid. Therefore 3♡ is an all-purpose game try bid, a first cousin to opener's double after

1♠   Pass   2♠   3♡
?

All distributional game tries bid 3♡, since the double of 3◊ is reserved for balanced game tries. Therefore after

1♠   Pass   2♠   3◊
?

bid 3♡ on each of the following:

♠ K Q 8 6 3   ♡ A Q 6 5   ◊ 8 4   ♣ A 7,

♠ A J 8 7 4 2   ♡ Q 7 4   ◊ 9   ♣ A Q 5

and even

♠ A K J 10 4   ♡ 8   ◊ 9 2   ♣ A J 8 7 4.

As you can see, 3♡ certainly does not promise hearts, and is therefore quite Alertable.

Sequences No. 10 (1♡ –2♣ –2♡ –3♣ –Dbl) and No. 11 (1♡ –2◊ –2♡ – 3◊ –Dbl) form a perfect parallel with #5, 6 and 7. Since we have some bidding room after 1♡ –2♣ –2♡ –3♣, double is a balanced game try and 3◊ shows an unbalanced game try, although the hand may or may not have diamond length. However, after

1♡   2◊   2♡   3◊
?

there is no maneuvering room at all, so all hands with possible game interest say "Double" just as you do after

1♠   Pass   2♠   3♡
?

This is another example of a maximal overcall double which certainly does complicate matters for opener's side.

12.   1♡   2♣   2♡   3♣
                 3◊

This sequence also has a parallel in a previous sequence (No. 9: 1♠ –Pass–2♠ –3◊ –3♡). We said that 3♡ is our only means of showing a distributional game try, and it should be apparent that the same is true of Auction 12. So bid 3◊ here not only with

♠ A 6   ♡ K J 8 7 5   ◊ A J 9 6 4   ♣ 8,

but also with

♠ K 10 7   ♡ A Q 10 6 5 3   ◊ K J 2   ♣ 8.

Let's sum up what we've said this far, keeping in mind that the suggestions made are definitely not the only way to approach these problems. After we open and single raise a major and the opponents overcall, the meaning of double and opener's new suit at the 3-level are dependent on the amount of bidding room remaining.

Use the following chart to help understand and remember the conditions stated earlier.

	Double	New Suit Bid (below 3 of agreed suit)	Return to 3 of our suit
A lot of room such as 1♠-P-2♠-3♣	Optional, balanced game try, can be left in	Length promised and game interest	Bar bid, showing weak hand with very good shape
Some room such as 1♠-P-2♠-3◊	Same as above	Distributional game try, may be artificial	Same as above
No room such as 1♠-P-2♠-3♡	Only game try available, rarely passed		Same as above

Now we will finish up with auctions that deal with what happens after the partnership has found a major suit fit.

13. 1♡ Pass 2♡ Pass
     3♡

This used to be an obvious invitational auction, but the modern philosophy is to use a new suit as a game try, which also serves to focus attention on a particular suit. If we accept that, we would bid 3◊ on

♠ A 6   ♡ A Q 7 4 2   ◊ A 6 4 3   ♣ J 7

and 3♣ with

♠ 9 4   ♡ K Q 8 7 4   ◊ A K   ♣ Q J 7 2

and 2 NT holding

♠ K 9 5   ♡ A 9 6 4 3   ◊ A 7   ♣ A J 6

(although it might have been a good idea to open 1 NT). It becomes clear that we really don't need 3♡ as a game try. Therefore 3♡ is used as a "bar bid," or a form of preempt. Imagine holding

♠ 9   ♡ A K Q J 4 2   ◊ Q 6   ♣ 9 7 3 2

and hearing your partner raise your 1♡ opening to 2♡. Don't you have a lot more offense than defense? Aren't you afraid that if you pass 2♡ the opponents might balance in spades and outbid you, possibly even to game? Do you think that if you pass 2♡ your LHO will decline to balance? Remember, the opponents must have a good fit in spades and/or diamonds with at least half the high cards in the deck.

The recommended action is to bid a preemptive 3 ♡ immediately, which should be high enough to keep out the opponents. 3 ♡ still preserves the chance of going plus, so a preemptive 4 ♡ would be over exuberant. Of course, 3 ♡ must be alerted as a "bar bid," (i.e., a weak bid showing no game interest).

Another common example of a bar bid might be

1 ♡	Pass	2 ♡	2 ♠
3 ♡			

where we are saying that all we wish to do is compete to a 3 ♡. With game interest we would bid a new suit or 2 NT.

We came across the bar bid concept in Auction 8

(1 ♠	Pass	2 ♠	3 ♡)
(3 ♠			)

and to some extent in Auction 3

(1 ♠	Pass	2 ♠	3 ◇)
(4 ♠			).

14.

1 ♡	Pass	2 ♡	2 ♠
4 ♣			

This auction is a throwback to Auction 2

(1 ♠	Pass	2 ♠	3 ◇)
(4 ♣			)

We are showing clubs and setting up a forcing auction, in case the opponents compete over 4 ♠. Since 3 ♠ would only be a game try, 4 ♣ is the only club bid that commits us to game.

15.

1 ♡	1 ♠	2 ♡	2 ♠
3 ♠			

The cuebid after we find a fit and the opponents compete promises a game forcing hand with no second suit and sets up a forcing pass auction. Our earlier example was Auction 4

(1 ♠	Pass	2 ♠	3 ◇)
(4 ◇			)

and the fact that both opponents have bid the suit doesn't really change anything.

16.

1 ♡	1 ♠	2 ♡	3 ♠
4 ♣			

Although this auction may strike you as being in the same class as Auction 14, Auction 16 merits more careful attention. The reason for this is the lack of alternatives. In addition, we no longer have a cuebid without committing the hand to the five-level, and we don't have any game tries available, since any bid commits you to game. The truth is, the opponent's 3 ♠ bid has taken away bidding room that could have been used very profitably. Well, what are our alternatives?

In addition to 4 ♡, the only alternatives to a new suit at the four-level are 3 NT and double, assuming that we're not going to pass. The double should be used with a good balanced hand. With

♠ K 7 4   ♡ A Q 9 6 3   ◇ A 5   ♣ K J 5,

make an *optional* double of 3 ♠, expecting partner to know whether to pass or bid 4 ♡.

As for 3 NT, it is very unlikely that we would ever be anxious to play 3 NT when we have bid and raised a major suit while the opponents have bid and raised a suit. Therefore 3 NT is free to be used as a fit bid. How about treating it as a good 4 ♡ bid, setting up a forcing auction like our cuebids would (when available)?

4 ♡ would then be simply a competitive bid, just like all game bids have been in our study of competitive auctions. 4 ♣ and 4 ◇ are now free to be used as second suits with good hands, which is what we have done when more bidding room was available. It is also helpful to retain the same meaning for bids, since specific understandings increase the possibility of memory problems and misunderstandings.

17.   1 ◇   1 ♡   1 ♠   2 ♡
                            Pass   3 ♡

For the first time in our "Dirty 1½ Dozen," We are the overcalling side. But the concepts and principles remain the same. If we were interested in game, we could easily bid 2 NT, 3 ♣, or even 3 ◇. Therefore 3 ♡ is our old friend, the bar bid. This is more urgently needed here than usual, since the probability of this hand belonging to the opponents is greater (their side not only opened the bidding but also responded). You should bid 3 ♡ with the following hands:

♠ 9   ♡ Q 10 7 6 4 3   ◇ K 6   ♣ K 10 7 4

♠ 9 4   ♡ K Q J 10 7   ◇ 8   ♣ K 10 7 4 2

♠ 7 4 2   ♡ A K 9 7 4 3   ◇ Q 10 6   ♣ 9

After all, you know that you won't be buying the contract for 2 ♡ with the above hands, unless your opponents have stopped breathing.

18.   1 ♣   Pass   1 ♡   1 ♠
                            2 ♡   Pass   3 ♡

This appears to be a bar bid auction, and indeed it should be. Just because the opponents have been fairly quiet so far doesn't mean they are through. Also, 3 ♡ is hardly needed as a game try, since we haven't been crowded and have 2 NT, 3 ♣ and 3 ◇ available as game tries. Picture having responded 1 ♡ on

♠ 9   ♡ K Q 10 6 4   ◇ 9 3 2   ♣ 10 8 7 4   or

♠ 9 3   ♡ K J 7 4 3 2   ◇ Q 8   ♣ 9 7 4

Don't you feel that you don't rate to buy the contract in $2\heartsuit$ but that nothing bad should happen to $3\heartsuit$?

I've heard people say that $3\heartsuit$ should be a game try promising a five-card suit, so that opener (holding a suitable maximum) can accept even with only three trumps. Although this idea has some merit, those of us who are enlightened enough to use "support doubles" have already learned that opener promised four hearts when he raised to $2\heartsuit$ over $1\spadesuit$. With a three-card raise we would double $1\spadesuit$. So perhaps the five-card suit game try should be reserved for an auction like

$1\clubsuit$	Pass	$1\heartsuit$	Pass
$2\heartsuit$	Pass	$3\heartsuit$	

where there was no intervention to allow us to distinguish between three or four-card raises.

Although we are finished with "18 auctions after a major suit fit," we still have some ground to cover as we strive to learn all we can about constructive and competitive bidding involving fits.

"Fits," Suits, or Splinters

We will now take a look at auctions where it is not so obvious whether bids should be regarded as "fits" or suits or splinters. Auctions involving passed hands are usually much more obvious because there are so many more negative inferences. Because of this the majority of our discussions will concentrate on auctions involving unpassed hands.

1. $1\heartsuit$ Dbl $4\clubsuit$

Most players would agree this is a splinter bid, showing an opening bid in support of hearts with club shortness. But is this practical? Even when the right hand occurs for this convention, I have never seen a hand where the bid accomplished anything. Opener always signs off in $4\heartsuit$, since chances for slam against a takeout double are almost nil. Doubler's side doesn't bid any more since fourth hand has a near yarborough. So what good does it do for opener to know of the club shortness if responder's hand almost certainly is going to be dummy in a heart game?

However, with a hand like

    $\spadesuit\,85$ $\heartsuit\,KJ94$ $\diamondsuit\,3$ $\clubsuit\,KJ8753,$

can't you see the urgency to convey information to opener? There is a good chance the opponents will compete in spades or diamonds. Don't we want partner to know of our clubs when he is deciding whether to bid on or defend? It is more likely that you will hold about 8 HCP after an opening bid and double than the equivalent of an opening bid. Needless to say, the logic for the fit interpretation would be stronger still if $4\clubsuit$ was bid by a passed hand.

2. $1\heartsuit$ $2\clubsuit$ $4\diamondsuit$

As in #1, this double jump to the four level can't be a natural one-suiter, so our choice is between a fit-bid and a splinter.

Most good players play this as a splinter – they would argue that chances for a slam are livelier after an overcall than after a takeout double, which is correct. However, my preference once again would be to regard 4 ◊ as a fit-bid. In some of my regular partnerships, I even go so far as to play *no splinters in competitive auctions, except into the opponent's suit.*

3.   1 ♣   Dbl   3 ♡

Here we clearly have three possible interpretations; natural, splinter, or fit. My "no splinters in competition" rule would eliminate that possibility for myself, and I never seem to have a good enough suit to jump to three after their takeout double, so once again I would treat this as a fit-showing bid. (You have to admit that I'm consistent, at least.) A possible hand would be

     ♠ 9   ♡ A 10 9 6 5   ◊ 4 3   ♣ K Q 10 8 7.

By the way, these length-showing fit-jumps are forcing if the opening bid was a major, not forcing if the opening bid was a minor. Therefore, opener could pass 3 ♡ with something like

     ♠ K Q 6 5   ♡ 7 3 2   ◊ K 6   ♣ A J 6 5,

where opener knows he has the wrong hand, while

                  1 ♡   Dbl   4 ♣ and

                  1 ♡   2 ♣   4 ◊ are

forcing to 4 ♡.

4.   1 ♣   1 ◊   3 ♡

This auction is similar to #3, although you could point out that responder is much more likely to have a long heart suit after an overcall as opposed to a takeout double. However, there are two reasons why I prefer to play 3 ♡ as a fit-bid.

First of all, 2 ♡ is available to show a preemptive heart hand. This "weak jump shift in competition" is played by virtually all top players. Secondly, I don't go out of my way to preempt when my side has opened, unless of course I have a big fit. If the 3 ♡ bidder was a passed hand, then the natural possibility would be removed, since any hand worth a natural 3 ♡ bid now should not have been passed earlier.

5.   1 ◊   1 ♠   4 ♡   or

                  1 ◊   Dbl   4 ♡

Even advocates of fit-bidding like myself have to bow to the inevitable sometimes. We must allow partner to jump to game with a long major suit. Therefore, these auctions are natural, perhaps based on a hand like

     ♠ 9   ♡ Q J 10 9 7 5 4 2   ◊ Q 7   ♣ 9 4.

4 ♡ would have to be a fit-bid if made by a passed hand, and although unlikely, the passed hand could hold

     ♠ 9   ♡ Q J 10 7 5   ◊ A J 9 7 4 3   ♣ 8

6.   1♡   2♣   3◇

I'm not convinced that it's wrong to play this as a fit-bid, showing a raise
to 3♡ with diamonds along with hearts like

         ♠ 9 4   ♡ K J 8 7   ◇ K Q 8 5 3   ♣ 10 4.

Clearly that's how I would treat 3◇ if bid by a passed hand, since a passed
hand should never have a long suit worth showing. However, I do play 3◇
as natural and preemptive if bid by an unpassed hand unless playing negative
free bids. There really is no other way to show a hand like

         ♠ K 8 4   ♡ 9 3   ◇ Q J 10 9 7 4 3   ♣ 5,

since partner will expect more high cards if you bid 2◇.

7.   Pass   Pass   1♣   Dbl
                      2♡

Once again most of the world would play this as natural and preemptive.
However, for those of us who like to preempt friskily, it is not clear why
we would wish to preempt now if our hand was not suitable for a preempt
as dealer. Therefore, 2♡ should show clubs and hearts.

As much as I favor fancy fit-bids in competition vs. traditional bids or even
modern splinter bids, we must not lose sight of the most important element
of a good partnership, which is knowing what partner's bids mean. The
danger in using nonstandard methods is that the partnership may concentrate more on have *good understandings* than on having a *good understanding*
of the methods. Nevertheless, without experimentation progress is
impossible.

Defining Some Ambiguous Auctions

We will now try to define some auctions where bridge logic may point
to the correct interpretation, but it wouldn't hurt to go deeper rather than
assume that everyone is on the same wavelength.

Do *all* players treat these auctions the same way? Probably not, but *most*
experts agree on *most* of these auctions which begin with notrump.

Since a fair number of these auctions begin with a notrump opening bid,
that's a reasonable place to start.

1.   1 NT   3♡
                      4♣

Although most pairs these days prefer Jacoby Transfers, there are players
who still use standard methods after notrump openings. 4♣ shows a good
raise to 4♡ with the ♣A. Presumably it denies the ♠A, since opener would
have cuebid 3♠ holding that card. There might be some disagreement as
to how good a raise opener needs in order to cuebid. Some would require
a maximum, while others would feel that the advanced cuebid (which certainly qualifies as a fit-bid) is in order even with only a fair raise to 4♡. Determining the standards for advanced cuebids is a necessity for a top pair, since
there are many auctions analogous to the above.

100

2.   1 NT   2♡ *
                3♣

*transfer

Since we could hardly go adventuring to the three-level to show a club suit not worth opening, 3♣ must be some sort of fit-bid in support of spades. Also, since responder could easily hold a hand like

♠ J 10 9 7 4   ♡ 8   ◊ 10 7 4 3   ♣ 8 6 2

opener must have a real rock. It is possible to treat 3♣ as the cheapest outside ace, but it is premature to worry about slam when responder hasn't even promised enough strength to be confident about making a partscore. Therefore, it is recommended that a new suit by opener show a doubleton, in addition to four plus spades and a tip-top notrump opening.

♠ A Q 8 5   ♡ A 9 7 3   ◊ K 9 5   ♣ A 5

would be a good example, although the bid would still be justified with a shade less. 3♡ by responder would be played by most as a retransfer, since you still want opener to be declarer. It's a good idea to discuss this with your favorite partners – you haven't lived until you've taken part in a "retransfer" auction when one player thinks he is retransferring – and the other doesn't!

3.   1 NT   2♣
                2♠   3♡

If this seems like an impossible auction using transfer bids, you are correct. Responder would raise spades with four spades and five hearts, and would have started with a transfer if holding five plus hearts and fewer than four spades. Therefore we play 3♡ as an artificial fit-showing bid promising spade support and a slam try. Neither 3♣ nor 3◊ can be used this way in most partnerships, since they are presumably needed to show certain kinds of minor suit hands.

4.   1 NT   2♣
                2♡   3♠

Other than a splinter bid, it's hard to imagine what this could possibly be. Actually, it is the counterpart to Auction 3. 3♠ here agrees hearts and suggests a slam, without showing anything special in spades.

5.   2 NT   3♣
                3♡   3♠

6.   2 NT   3♣
                3♠   4♡

These, of course, are the 2 NT equivalents of Auctions 3 and 4. Once again they represent idle auctions to which we are more than willing to assign meanings. They are economical ways to show support and suggest slam.

7.   1 NT   2♡
                2♠   4◊

This sequence features an unnecessary jump by responder. Since 3 ◊ would be forcing, 4 ◊ is played as a 6-3-1-3 hand with slam interest.

♠ A Q 8 6 4 3   ♡ K J 7   ◊ 8   ♣ K 9 5

is a reasonable example. Opener is requested to evaluate his hand in view of that information, keeping in mind that diamond strength represents duplication opposite responder's singleton. Spades is assumed to be the trump suit, but opener can even bid a slam in one of responder's fragment suits with a hand like

♠ 7 2   ♡ A 10 4   ◊ A 5 3   ♣ A Q J 10 7.

While we're on the subject of splinter bids, two other auctions are worthy of mention.

8.   1♣   1 NT
                       3♡

9.   1♣   1♠
                       3♡

Both of these "jump reverse" auctions show shortness in hearts. A simple 2♡ bid would be forcing showing a heart suit. Of course, there's nothing inherently special regarding hearts—a jump to 3 ◊ by opener would convey the same meaning. The jump in Auction 8 shows a good 3-1-3-6 hand, with game interest even opposite a 1 NT response. It warns responder about hearts for notrump while reassuring him about spades and diamonds. Although it is possible for the partnership to stop in 4♣, this auction is normally game-forcing.

♠ A J 5   ♡ 9   ◊ A 10 6   ♣ A K J 8 7 4

qualifies nicely.

The jump reverse in Auction 9 can help portray the kind of hand that is close to impossible to describe using standard methods. If you open 1♣ with

♠ A K 7 4   ♡ 5   ◊ A 8 5   ♣ A K J 7 4

and get a pleasant surprise when partner responds 1♠, what now? A reverse to 2 ◊ is forcing, but it certainly doesn't show a monstrous spade raise. You could offer a splinter raise by bidding 4♡, but you couldn't expect partner to be enthusiastic with

♠ Q 9 6 5 3   ♡ Q 7 4 2   ◊ 6 2   ♣ Q 6.

We refer to the big hand as a five-level raise, requesting that partner go on to slam with just a useful card or two. We use the jump reverse as a raise to the five-level *or* a raise to the three-level—a minisplinter with shortness in hearts. It should be easy enough to sort out one from the other, as long as the partners are careful. Responder assumes that opener has the three-level raise but will hear loud and clear from opener when the "big surprise" is held.

Fit Bids Involving Minor Suits

Although most of our fit bid auctions have dealt with major suits, there are also some interesting possibilities that can arise after a minor suit is agreed. What do you think these mean?

1.	1♣	2♣
	2♡	2♠
2.	1♣	2♣
	3♢	
3.	1♣	2♣
	2♡	3♣
	3♢	

In each case, opener has enough strength to continue even though responder only could make a single raise.

After 1♣–2♣, 2♡ is a one-round force, showing a very good hand with a side four-card heart suit. Responder is expected to bid 3♣ with a minimum and to make a descriptive call with a good 2♣ bid. 2♠, therefore, shows spade values, with a non-minimum raise. Responder can't have a spade suit, since his 2♣ bid denies a four-card major. For example:

♠ 8	♠ K Q 10
♡ A 8 4 3	♡ J 7 2
◇ A Q	◇ 8 6 4
♣ A K 9 7 4 2	♣ Q J 6 5
1♣	2♣
2♡	2♠

Opener would now jump to 3 NT. Good bidding to a good contract.

In auction (2), opener's jump to 3◇ is a splinter bid. He must have a very good three-suited hand with at most one diamond.

♠ A K 7 4   ♡ A Q 9 3   ◇ 8   ♣ A J 6 4

would be about right. Responder should bid 3 NT with

♠ Q 6   ♡ 7 4 2   ◇ K Q 10   ♣ 10 7 4 3 2,

5♣ holding

♠ J 6   ♡ 10 2   ◇ J 7 5 3   ♣ K Q 10 9 3,

and 4♣ (nonforcing) on

♠ J 5 2   ♡ 7 4   ◊ Q J 2   ♣ Q 9 5 3 2.

On auction (3), opener is still trying hard despite responder's lack of enthusiasm. The 3 ◊ bid should show a *fragment* (usually three) and suggest very few spades.

♠ J   ♡ A K 7 3   ◊ K Q 5   ♣ A J 10 7 4

is a possibility, hoping that partner can appreciate *the fit* and jump to 5♣ on

♠ 10 7 4   ♡ 9 2   ◊ J 10 6   ♣ K Q 8 3 2.

While we're on the subject of minor suit fit auctions, let's try a few more. However, as we're about to see, some of these fits may not be as minor as the first glance might indicate!

4.	1 ◊	1 ♠
	4 ◊	
5.	1 ♣	1 ♡
	1 ♠	4 ♣
6.	1 ◊	1 NT
	2 ◊	2 ♠
7.	1 ♣	1 NT
	2 ♠	3 ◊
8.	1 ◊	1 ♠
	2 ♣	4 ♣

On auction (4), opener has made a majestic double jump to four of his original minor. Very few jumps to four of a minor by opener are natural, since we invariably try for 3 NT first. So instead of playing this as a freakish one-suiter, it is a spade raise with long diamonds (usually 4–6 in the two suits). Obviously, it shows a very good hand, since we are forcing to game. I would happily bid this holding

♠ A J 7 4   ♡ 9 4   ◊ K Q J 6 4 2   ♣ A.

Auction (5) features another double jump to four of a minor. If responder had such great clubs, he could either jump to 3♣ or bid 2 ◊ (fourth suit forcing) and follow it up with a club bid. Therefore, the direct leap to 4♣ is a splinter bid! This is Alertable, as is 4 ◊ on (4). It shows a good spade raise with club shortness, relevant even after the opening 1♣ bid. If the two hands were

♠ A Q J 6	♠ K 10 9 7
♡ K 7	♡ A Q 8 5
◊ 9 2	◊ A 6 4 3
♣ A 8 7 4 2	♣ 6

4♣ would be the key bid leading to an excellent 6♠ on only 27 HCP's.

On auction (6), like auction (4), responder is up to his old tricks again, bidding a major after he denied one with his 1 NT response! What responder is up to, of course, is showing spade values on the way to 3 ◊. This would allow us to intelligently bid a cold 3 NT with

♠ 9		♠ A K 6
♡ J 7 5 2	opposite	♡ 9 4 3
◊ A K J 7 4 2		◊ Q 6 5
♣ A 8		♣ 10 9 4 2

Will you also grant that responder can't have a great diamond suit after he responds 1 NT to 1 ♣, so 3 ◊ on auction (7) must be a fit bid? Since 1 ♣ – 1 NT denies a major, the fit must be in clubs. Therefore, opener should expect something like

♠ Q 7 4   ♡ 9 4 3   ◊ A Q J   ♣ J 7 4 2

across the table, and proceed accordingly.

Auction (8), our last for now, features an almost unheard of occurrence in 1985: a natural sequence involving no Alerts!! It is also noteworthy because of the forcing second round jump by responder, which is unusual for most adherents of fourth suit forcing. Also, as stated earlier, natural jumps to four of a minor are rare. Responder has a huge club fit (to explain going past 3 NT) with at least ten black cards. Opener is urged to cuebid in search of slam. Responder could have

♠ A Q 7 4 2   ♡ 9 4   ◊ 9   ♣ A Q 6 4 3.

We've really come full circle now. Imagine a fit bid involving a direct raise of partner's suit without any frills! Don't worry, readers, it's not likely to happen again!

Cuebids

For many years now, the surest road to a good score in *The Bridge World's* Master Solvers' Club has been to cuebid. Of course in real life you would have to figure out what to do next, but in 1986 it is safe to assume that those who "when in doubt, cuebid" will never find themselves alone on a limb.

Now we will look at two kinds of competitive cuebids, some of which promise a fit for partner while others only guarantee a good hand.

Since some of these cuebids guarantee a fit, while others do not, is there one key which will be the determining factor?

The answer is definitely *yes*. Whenever we do not have a convenient low-level forcing bid available, the cuebid will have to be used as the only force, with or without a fit. On the other hand, if we have a way to force while lacking a fit, then we can reserve the cuebid for good hands which contain one.

Before proceeding further, let's pause for a moment to illustrate the above rule.

(1) After 1♢ – 1♡ – Dbl (neg.) – Pass, there is no way for opener to force other than a 2♡ cuebid. Both 2♠ and 3♣ are invitational, just like a jump to 3♢. At least that's the way most people respond to negative doubles. Since 2♡ is opener's only forcing bid, the cuebid says nothing about how opener feels about responder's spades. Opener should cuebid with

♠ A 6   ♡ 5   ♢ A K Q J 7 4   ♣ A J 9 3

as well as with

♠ A Q 5 4   ♡ A 6   ♢ K Q J 7 4   ♣ K 5.

(2) However, after 1♡ – Pass – 2♣ – 3♢, not only would opener's bid of 3♡ or 3♠ be forcing, but he could even force responder to act by passing! Therefore, opener's 4♢ cuebid must show a big club raise. With any other big hand, opener would look for a fit at the three-level.

Now we're ready to take a look at some cuebid auctions while checking for fits. If we polled a panel of experts on these auctions their only agreement would be that they disagreed on most! We'll begin with some cuebids where a fit is guaranteed.

(3) 1♡ – 2♠ – 3♠. Responder's cuebid promises hearts and is absolutely forcing to game. A spade control is not required, but responder should have a good forcing raise. With a limit raise or an ugly forcing raise like

♠ Q 6   ♡ A Q 7 4   ♢ Q 6 4   ♣ Q J 5 3

responder can jump to 4♡ (not preemptive) since the opponent's preempt has taken away some of his options. Notice that responder has lots of alternatives with a good hand lacking heart support. He can negative double, bid three of a minor, or bid 3 NT with good spade stoppers.

(4) 1♢ – 2♠ – 3♠. This guarantees support for opener's suit. There are lots of bids available for good responding hands lacking diamonds. Clearly opener will be anxious to bid 3 NT if possible. But if opener can't bid 3 NT, can we stop in 4♢? Also, is it possible to play in 4♡?

I would say that it is possible for us to stop in 4♢ if responder has something like

♠ 6 4 3   ♡ A K 7 5   ♢ A J 7 3   ♣ 8 2

and opener has

♠ 9 5   ♡ Q 7   ♢ K Q 10 6 4   ♣ A Q 5 3.

There is little point in being forced to 5♢ when we can be sure from the auction that it will have no play.

While the cuebid guarantees diamond support, responder might have four hearts. I would certainly bid 3♠ holding

♠ 6 5   ♡ Q 7 4 2   ◇ A K Q 10 6 4   ♣ 8.

It's even possible that we would want to play 4♡ with a 4–3 fit. It would be the only game if responder holds

♠ 8 7 4   ♡ A Q 10 6   ◇ K Q J 5   ♣ 6 3

opposite

♠ 9 3   ♡ K J 8   ◇ A 10 7 4 3   ♣ A J 4.

But as a general rule I would say that 4♡ by either player (after 1◇–2♣–3♠) was a cuebid, with diamonds the agreed suit.

(5) 1◇–1♠–3♠. This jump cuebid also agrees diamonds, and would be played by most as a splinter bid, promising 0–1 spades. Should a 4◇ rebid by opener be forcing in this case? I would say yes, since responder went out of his way to jump to 3♠. If responder had only a marginal hand like

♠ 8   ♡ Q 7 4   ◇ A K J 7 4   ♣ J 7 5 3

he might have bid 2♠ earlier, a limit raise plus, which wouldn't have committed the partnership to a game.

By the way, although my opinions on auctions (4) and (5) seem logical to me, it is possible that some players' views differ from mine. That's why partnership discussion is so crucial. There are too many obscure auctions where a meeting of the minds is unlikely to occur by itself.

(6) 2◇–2♠–Pass–3♠. When the opponents preempt and we overcall, a new suit by an unpassed hand should be forcing below game. If a forcing three-of-a-minor is available for responder, then 3♡ is free to be a good spade raise—our old friend, the limit raise or better. If 3♠ would be bid on

♠ Q 7 4 3   ♡ 8 2   ◇ A J 10 6   ♣ 9 4 3,

then 3♡ should promise a better hand for spades, at least

♠ A J 6   ♡ 7 5 4 3   ◇ A 6   ♣ 9 5 4 3 or

♠ 6 4 2   ♡ 7 5 4   ◇ K Q J 6   ♣ A J 5

So much for cuebids which promise a fit. But not all cuebids are that definitive. Next we'll check out some "fuzzy–wuzzy" cuebids where there is no way of anyone knowing what suit we have in mind until we reveal our intentions with our rebid.

Cuebids, Once Again

Although cuebids usually promise a fit, there are times where this just isn't practical. The two most likely situations for this to occur are:
(1) When non-cuebids would not be forcing or
(2) We need the cuebid as a notrump probe.
Even experts are unable to agree on the meaning of competitive cuebids. Consider this auction:

$$1\clubsuit \qquad 1\heartsuit \qquad \text{Pass} \qquad 3\clubsuit .$$

Most would say 3♣ promises a heart fit, but even that would not be universally agreed. Some would say the jump to 3♣ should show a very good club suit, say ♣ K Q J 10 8 4. After all, if 2♣ is not available as a natural club bid, maybe 3♣ should be.

Even when we restrict our discussion to those who agree 3♣ guarantees hearts, we're still dealing with assorted interpretations. I've encountered each of the following:
(1) Mini Splinter, perhaps

$$\spadesuit \text{ A 8 7 4} \qquad \heartsuit \text{ A 5 4 2} \qquad \diamondsuit \text{ 9 6 4 3} \qquad \clubsuit \text{ 8}$$

(2) Limit Raise, allowing the 2♣ cuebid to show a good hand without hearts.
(3) Limit Raise + with club length, so the partnership can get to 3 NT instead of 4♡ when overcaller has the appropriate holding, such as J 7 4 2, Q J 3, or even 9 7 4 3.
(4) My preference, the "Mixed Raise." This shows a hand too good for a weak jump raise, but not enough high cards for a limit-raise-or-better cuebid.

Here are some auctions where a cuebid doesn't promise a fit.

1.   1♣   Pass   1♠   2♡
            3♡

Yes, opener should bid this way with

$$\spadesuit \text{ A K 8 3} \qquad \heartsuit \text{ A 6} \qquad \diamondsuit \text{ K 5} \qquad \clubsuit \text{ K Q 9 7 2,}$$

to distinguish this hand from the one that jumps to 4♣ in competition such as

$$\spadesuit \text{ A Q 10 6} \qquad \heartsuit \text{ 8 5} \qquad \diamondsuit \text{ 6} \qquad \clubsuit \text{ K Q J 10 7 4.}$$

However, don't we also have to cuebid 3♡ with

$$\spadesuit \text{ A Q} \qquad \heartsuit \text{ 9 4 2} \qquad \diamondsuit \text{ K 5} \qquad \clubsuit \text{ A K Q J 7 4?}$$

We'd like to get to 3 NT with this hand, but can hardly bid it ourselves without a stopper in the opponent's suit. Therefore, responder must temporarily assume that opener is looking for 3 NT with a great club suit, and opener will always pull 3 NT with a hand with primary spade support. We shall see in subsequent examples that the primary responsibility after a three-level cuebid often is to bid 3 NT with a stopper. If partner has bigger and better things in mind, he can now clarify his intentions.

2.   2♠   3♢   Pass   3♡
            Pass   3♣

It is certainly possible that the overcaller has

♠ A 6   ♡ K 7 4   ◇ K J 10 7 4 2   ♣ A 8

and would like to show the spade control on the way to 4 ♡. But responder must not assume that and bid 4 ♡ holding something like

♠ K 7 4   ♡ A Q J 8 3   ◇ 9 3   ♣ Q 5 4.

The 3 ◇ bidder could hold

♠ 8 5   ♡ 9 4   ◇ A K Q 10 7 4 2   ♣ K 7

and be looking for 3 NT, which might be our last plus score.

Because it is so easy to get into trouble if partners are on different wavelengths, let's illustrate how the bidding should go with East's hand opposite the two sample West hands.

WEST	NORTH	EAST	SOUTH
			2 ♠
3 ◇	Pass	3 ♡	Pass
3 ♠	Pass	3 NT	Pass
4 ♡	All Pass		

♠ A 6	♠ K 7 4
♡ K 7 4	♡ A Q J 8 3
◇ K J 10 7 4 2	◇ 9 3
♣ A 8	♣ Q 5 4

WEST	NORTH	EAST	SOUTH
			2 ♠
3 ◇	Pass	3 ♡	Pass
3 ♠	Pass	3 NT	All Pass

♠ 8 5	♠ K 7 4
♡ 9 4	♡ A Q J 8 3
◇ A K Q 10 7 4 2	◇ 9 3
♣ K 7	♣ Q 5 4

By the way, I strongly advise that East's 3 ♡ response be treated as forcing. I don't necessarily recommend that new suits should always be forcing opposite overcalls, but when we have overcalled a preempt, all unpassed-hand new suits should clearly be forcing below game.

3.   1 ♡   3 ◇   Dbl   Pass
             4 ◇

Double is negative here and most experienced players do play negative doubles at least this high. Responder has promised 4 + spades, although no one should criticize a double with

♠ K Q J   ♡ Q 8   ◇ J 3   ♣ K 10 7 4 3 2.

4 ♣ is hardly the bid of the year with this hand and we have too much to pass.

Opener's cuebid of 4♦ certainly doesn't agree spades – he could jump to 4♠ on a nice hand with four spades. 4♦ merely shows a hand strong enough to force to game, unsuitable for 3 NT or an immediate leap to 4♡, 4♠, or 5♣. Usually opener will have a good hand that lacks direction, although sometimes he will be angling for slam. Opener should bid 4♦ with

♠ A K 9   ♡ A Q 10 6 5   ◇ 9   ♣ K J 7 4 or

♠ A Q   ♡ Q 8 7 4 3 2   ◇ Q 5   ♣ A K J or

♠ K 7   ♡ A J 8 5 4   ◇ 9   ♣ A K J 7 4.

The need of the cuebid for so many hand types, of course, is that bids like 3♡, 3♠, and 4♣ are all nonforcing.

More Cuebids

The key to determining whether a cuebid opposite an overcall promises a fit is to consider the nature of a non-cuebid.

All of the auctions below contain cuebids that suggest a fit, but in some of the problem hands we will see that the overcaller can't always be guaranteed that a fit is present.

We will discover that many of these "probably a fit, but might not be" cuebids are looking for a notrump contract but the cuebidder lacks stoppers in the opponents' suit.

Take a look at the following auctions:

1.	2♠	3♡	Pass	3♠
2.	2♡	2♠	Pass	3♡
3.	2♡	3◇	Pass	3♡

In each case the opponents have opened with a *weak two-bid* and our side has overcalled and cuebid their suit. It would seem that the degree of fit promised is equivalent for each auction, but that is not true. Suppose fourth hand holds an opening bid with a good club suit but can't bid 3 NT (no stopper) and lacks support for overcaller's suit. On auctions (1) and (3) there is no choice – fourth hand must cuebid to give the partnership a chance to play in notrump. However on the second auction, fourth hand has lots of room, so will bid 3♣ (forcing after we overcall their preempt). *You should show your good suit when you can.*

Please also note that while there is room on auction (2) for fourth hand to show either of the unbid suits, auction (3) allows responder to bid a spade suit (instead of 3♡) below 3 NT. On the first auction, responder has no convenient bidding space available.

In summary, on our second sample auction (2♡ –2♠ –Pass–3♡), responder is *guaranteeing* a fit with the cuebid. He would be able to do something else with a good hand lacking a fit. Neither of the cuebids on auctions (1) and (3) need be based on fits, especially on the first auction where there was exactly one bid available below 3 NT. Of course if responder *does* have a big fit, it will certainly be revealed at the next turn.

4.   1♡   Dbl   Pass   2♣
         Pass   2♡

Clearly the doubler has a big hand as the 2♣ bidder never promised any strength. It is likely that the cuebidder has a good fit in clubs. He already promised club support by doubling and needs a place to play opposite a Yarborough like

♠ 9 4   ♡ 8 5 4 2   ◇ 9 7 6   ♣ 10 7 4 3.

It is also true that the doubler would bid a suit now with a good hand and a five-card or longer suit with fewer than four clubs. However, there are some definite problem hands.

a.   ♠ A K J 6   ♡ 9 4   ◇ A K Q 5   ♣ A 7 4

b.   ♠ A Q 7 3   ♡ 8 6 4   ◇ A K J   ♣ A K 10

c.   ♠ A Q J 9   ♡ A 7   ◇ A K Q 5 2   ♣ Q 5

d.   ♠ A K Q J 5   ♡ 9 4   ◇ A K Q J   ♣ 8 7

I believe most experts would cuebid 2♡ after doubling on these hands. That doesn't mean they would be happy about it. If responder doesn't bid notrump, they will probably not be well placed. Anyway, that's why the cuebid on this auction *doesn't guarantee* a fit.

5.   1♡   2♣   2♠   Pass
         3♣

This auction might be a problem for many partnerships since it is not clear how far the partnership was forced after the 2♠ bid. Opener's 3♣ cuebid should be game forcing with many hand types possible. Opener might cuebid 3♣ on any of these hands:

e.   ♠ A 6   ♡ K Q 10 7 4 2   ◇ A 5   ♣ A 6 3

Too good for 3♡.

f.   ♠ A K 5   ♡ A Q J 7 4   ◇ A 6 5   ♣ 8 4

Too good for any spade raise.

g.   ♠ A J   ♡ K Q 10 6 4   ◇ A Q   ♣ 8 6 4 2

No other choice.

h.   ♠ A 5   ♡ A K 8 7 4   ◇ A J 6 5   ♣ 9 4

3◇, if it is forcing, but are you positive *that it is?*
Notice that only one of the above examples included a *fit*.

6.   1◇   1♠   Pass   2◇ or
         1♡   2♣   Pass   2♡.

Should this cuebid guarantee support? Most players would say yes, advising that one should not cuebid without support. But if a new suit is not forcing, and if a jump shift is not forcing, partner may have no forcing bid available

111

holding a great hand with a good suit of his own. Although it does seem that this can't be too efficient, experience has shown that it's not really a problem, since a game force lacking a fit is so rare, particularly opposite what could be a light overcall. Of course, some players treat a new suit as forcing opposite an overcall by an unpassed hand. Their problem occurs after an auction like

1♡   2♣   Pass   ?

One would be uneasy holding

♠ K J 10 9 6 4   ♡ 8 7 3   ◊ 6 4 2   ♣ 9,

faced with the alternative of passing 2♣ or forcing the bidding higher when your hand is so terrible for anything but a low-level spade partscore. Therefore, new suit forcing players would clearly say that a cuebid does promise support since we could have bid a suit with a good hand lacking a fit. The rest of us will have to make up our own minds, with my recommendation being that you should cuebid only when you do have a fit; otherwise don't worry about it.

The Good-Bad 2 NT

If we consider modern bidding, one inescapable conclusion is that auctions are becoming more and more competitive. Even new players are "getting in there" with weak two-bids, weak jump overcalls, overcalls on four-card suits, etc., trying to make the opponents guess. Common sense dictates that we need weapons to fight back.

Lebensohl, one of the most popular gadgets of the Seventies, is a good example of a convention which attempts to overcome interference. In exchange for giving up 2 NT as a natural bid, we gain a vehicle for showing both weak and strong hands. Lebensohl also may be played after we make a takeout double of an enemy weak two-bid.

But if the concept behind Lebensohl is a sound one, why restrict ourselves to just these two types of auctions? Aren't there many more occasions where we'd like to let partner know whether we are "good" or "bad?"

For example, have you ever been faced with a decision like this?

WEST	NORTH	EAST	SOUTH
	1◊	1♠	Dbl
2♠	3♡	Pass	?

♠ 6 4 3
♡ A 10 6 4
◊ J 7
♣ A 9 6 5

If partner is minimum, with, say:

♠ 8 5
♡ K Q 7 5
♢ A K 5 3
♣ 10 7 2

you are quite high enough already. But if partner has a better 3♡ bid:

♠ 8
♡ K Q 9 3
♢ K Q 10 6 4
♣ K 10 3

you will miss a good game if you pass.

Another common type of problem may occur on a hand like:

♠ A 10 8 6 4
♡ A 7 3
♢ J 4
♣ 10 9 4

WEST	NORTH	EAST	SOUTH
	1♢	1♡	1♠
2♡	3♢	Pass	?

3 NT is tempting, and would be laydown if partner had a nice hand like:

♠ Q 5
♡ 9 4
♢ A K Q 10 7 2
♣ A 3 2.

But if partner were only competing (and who could blame him) with:

♠ Q 3
♡ 9 2
♢ K Q 10 8 7 6 2
♣ A J

you need to stop at 3♢. Is there a solution? Sure! – All you have to do is employ the Lebensohl concept once again.

The following idea was first mentioned to me about five years ago by an expert from Chicago, where it had gained a following. The idea was to bid 2 NT on the good hands. Partner would generally relay with 3♣ (a la Lebensohl) and now we could name the suit in which we wanted to suggest extra values. (This could be thought of as "Reverse Lebensohl," since in the usual version of Lebensohl, 2 NT suggested the weaker type of hand.)

When we first tried this out, however, we found that further competition from the opponents often made life difficult; we were prevented from clarifying the nature of our hand at the three level. Therefore, we eventually defined 2 NT as the *weaker*, competitive bid, with the direct raise or suit rebid promising more. If the opponents might cause us to lose our fit, better we should risk this on our weak hands. We named this the "Good-Bad 2 NT," as opposed to "Lebensohl #3" or the equivalent.

We set up the following rules to govern Good-Bad 2 NT:

(1) The auction was at the two level.

(2) Right-hand opponent must have bid, doubled or redoubled.

When those two conditions were met, a direct bid at the three level would promise extra values (but was not forcing), while 2 NT would show a hand only worth a competitive move. The 2 NT bidder might be planning to compete in any suit, but he could not be about to reverse (since his 2 NT denied extra values). The partner of the Good-Bad 2 NT bidder would usually bid 3♣ as requested, but common sense sometimes would dictate another action. Holding:

> ♠ A
> ♡ K J 9 6
> ◇ K Q J 6 4 3
> ♣ 5 2

after:

WEST	NORTH	EAST	SOUTH
		2♠	Dbl
Pass	2 NT (1)	Pass	?

South clearly should rebid 3◇, not 3♣, since he can't risk having partner pass 3♣. With:

> ♠ 8 6 4
> ♡ K J 8 5
> ◇ K 10 6 2
> ♣ J 5

after:

WEST	NORTH	EAST	SOUTH
	1◇	1♠	Dbl
2♠	2 NT	Pass	?

South also would bid 3◇, since if partner has a minor two-suiter he wants to play in diamonds. If North was about to bid hearts he can still do so.

Also, you must not lazily bid 3♣ with a good hand. After:

WEST	NORTH	EAST	SOUTH
	1◇	Pass	1♠
2♡	2 NT	Pass	?

bid 3♡ with:

> ♠ A K 10 6 3
> ♡ 9 3
> ◇ K 10 4
> ♣ K 6 3,

114

and 3 NT with:

$$♠ \text{ A } 10\ 9\ 4$$
$$♡ \text{ K Q } 10$$
$$◊ \text{ } 8\ 3$$
$$♣ \text{ A } 6\ 4\ 3$$

just as you would have if partner had rebid a "standard" three-of-a-minor.

As helpful as Good-Bad rated to be (and was), we found there were auctions where it couldn't be used. For example, after a 1♡ opening and 2◊ overcall, 2 NT by responder must be natural and invitational – otherwise there is no way to handle:

$$♠ \text{ } 6\ 4\ 3$$
$$♡ \text{ A } 10$$
$$◊ \text{ K J } 6$$
$$♣ \text{ Q } 10\ 6\ 4\ 3.$$

So we had to come up with a list of Good-Bad 2 NT exceptions. They are:

1. When 2 NT must be natural and invitational
2. When 2 NT clearly would be Unusual
3. When either side opens 1 NT
4. When the opponents open with a strong and forcing 1♣.
5. When either side opens with a weak two-bid
6. When a Good-Bad auction is illogical because the opponents are known to be very strong or our side is known to be very weak.
7. When the opponents make a penalty double.
8. When they use a convention at the two level against which we employ a predetermined defense.
9. When we bid a suit, then raise (possibly with a cuebid, implying a fit). Once a fit has been found, it is easy to distinguish preemptive reraises from invitational bids.
10. When we already are in a game-forcing auction.
11. When we made a preemptive jump.

Note that Good-Bad exceptions arise for either of two reasons: we've already determined which side owns the hand (4, 6, 7, 10, 11), or we must not interfere with agreements (conventional or not) that are already in place (1, 2, 3, 5, 8, 9). Of course, the conventional agreement for #3 and #5 may well be Lebensohl itself.

One last thought. Since further enemy competition may cause a suit to be lost after the "Bad" 2 NT bid, when faced with a close decision you should prefer the "Good" three-level suit bid. You may not be sure whether:

$$♠ \text{ } 6\ 4$$
$$♡ \text{ A Q J } 10\ 7\ 4$$
$$◊ \text{ } 9\ 2$$
$$♣ \text{ } 10\ 5\ 3$$

is worth a good 3♡ after: 1♠ –2◊ –2♠, but you would prefer 3♡ to 2 NT since you might never be able to show hearts if the opponents bid 3♠ over 2 NT.

Before we look at a few examples, let me answer a question which may have occurred to some – is 2 NT Good-Bad 100% forcing? Since notrump may be the last thing on partner's mind, I wouldn't advise passing it. However, on rare occasions passing may be a reasonable shot. Suppose the auction begins:

WEST	NORTH	EAST	SOUTH
1♣	1♠	Pass	2♠
2 NT	Pass	?	

and you gaze at:

> ♠ K J 10 8
> ♡ 8 7 4 3
> ◊ 9 6 5 4 2
> ♣ —

Partner must intend to play in clubs, since, as we stated last month, the 2 NT bidder can never be planning to reverse. If you'd rather play 2 NT than table this hand as dummy in 3♣, pass and hope for the best.

Recently I held:

> ♠ K Q 10
> ♡ —
> ◊ 10 8 7 4 3
> ♣ Q 9 6 4 2

and the auction went:

WEST	NORTH	EAST	SOUTH
Pass	Pass	1♡	1♠
Dbl	2♠	2 NT	Pass
?			

I chose to pass (nervously), assuming that partner was planning to rebid hearts and not a minor. This went down one while 3♡ would have been down three (possibly doubled). Partner had:

> ♠ 8 4
> ♡ A K 10 8 7 4
> ◊ A Q
> ♣ 10 7 3

so we survived with an above-average matchpoint score. But partner wouldn't have been too pleased with me if he had held:

> ♠ 8 4
> ♡ A Q J 7 4
> ◊ 2
> ♣ K J 8 5 3

and we went minus in 2 NT, cold for 4♣.

Try the following examples to test your knowledge of Good-Bad 2 NT.

(A)

WEST	NORTH	EAST	SOUTH
1♠	2♢	2♠	?

♠ A 8 5
♡ K 6 3
♢ Q 8 4 3
♣ 8 7 4

3♢. This is a good raise. Without the heart king, bid 2 NT.

(B)

WEST	NORTH	EAST	SOUTH
			1♢
1♠	Pass	2♢	?

♠ J
♡ K 10
♢ A K Q J 7 4 2
♣ 6 4 3

Bid 2 NT. We're not embarrassed about our diamonds, but we certainly don't want to encourage a partner to get involved when he couldn't take any action earlier (unless he had a penalty double of 1♠, of course). With another ace we would bid 3♢, allowing partner to bid 3 NT with:

♠ K 5 4 2
♡ Q 8 6
♢ 10 6
♣ J 7 5 2.

(C)

WEST	NORTH	EAST	SOUTH
			1♢
1♠	Dbl	2♠	?

♠ J
♡ K 10
♢ A K Q J 7 4 2
♣ 6 4 3

Bid 3♢, since not much is needed to make 3 NT opposite a partner who acted voluntarily.

(D)

WEST	NORTH	EAST	SOUTH
1♠	Dbl	2♠	?

♠ 8 7 4
♡ 6 3
♢ K 5 4
♣ Q J 10 8 5

Bid 2 NT. You are willing to compete, but you don't want to encourage partner.

(E)	WEST	NORTH	EAST	SOUTH
				1 ◊
	Pass	2 ♡	2 ♠	?

♠ 6 3
♡ A 8
◊ K Q J 8 6 5
♣ Q 8 5

Bid 3 ◊, not 2 NT. Good-Bad doesn't exist when a game force has been established.

(F)	WEST	NORTH	EAST	SOUTH
				1 ◊
	1 ♠	2 ♡	2 ♠	?

♠ K 6 3
♡ A 8
◊ A 9 4 3
♣ Q 8 7 5

Don't bid 2 NT even if you think the hand is worth it – 2 NT is not natural. This is a Good-Bad situation.

(G)	WEST	NORTH	EAST	SOUTH
				1 ♣
	1 ♠	1 NT	2 ♠	?

♠ 8
♡ 9 4
◊ A J 5 2
♣ A Q 10 7 4 3

Bid 2 NT, preparing to sign off in clubs. The fact that partner bid notrump earlier is not relevant.

(H)	WEST	NORTH	EAST	SOUTH
		1 ◊	Pass	1 NT
	Dbl	Pass	2 ♡	?

♠ 8 2
♡ 7 4
◊ A 5 3
♣ Q J 9 8 7 4

Bid 2 NT, preparing a club signoff. Again, the earlier notrump bid is not relevant.

(I)	WEST	NORTH	EAST	SOUTH
				1 NT
	Pass	2 ◇ (1)	2 ♠	?

(1) transfer

♠ 8 5
♡ A K 10 6
◇ A 7 4
♣ K J 8 5

Bid 3 ♡, even if you consider this a minimum. There is no Good-Bad 2 NT after 1 NT openings.

Now try responding to partner's Good-Bad 2 NT.

(A)	WEST	NORTH	EAST	SOUTH
		1 ♠	Pass	1 NT
	2 ♡	2 NT	Pass	?

♠ 10
♡ A J 7 4 3
◇ 9 8 5 4 2
♣ K 7

Bid 3 ♣. Partner has spades and a minor. If his minor is clubs, you hope he has five. If he converts to diamonds, you can raise.

(B)	WEST	NORTH	EAST	SOUTH
		1 ◇	1 ♠	Pass
	2 ♠	2 NT	Pass	?

♠ Q 8 5 4 3
♡ 8 7 4 3 2
◇ 9 5
♣ J

Bid 3 ◇, not 3 ♣. Regardless of whether partner has minors or only diamonds, you wish to play in his first suit.

(C)	WEST	NORTH	EAST	SOUTH
				1 ◇
	Pass	1 ♡	1 ♠	Dbl (1)
	2 ♠	2 NT	Pass	?

(1) support double, showing three hearts

♠ A 6 3 2
♡ A 7 4
◇ A 8 6 4
♣ 8 5

Bid 3 ♣. 2 NT is Good-Bad, and support doubles aren't on the list of exceptions. Isn't this a logical way to end in 3 ♣ when partner holds:

♠ 8
♡ J 9 7 3
◊ K 5
♣ Q J 10 9 4 2 2?

(D)	WEST	NORTH	EAST	SOUTH
		1♣	Pass	1♠
	2♡	2 NT	Pass	?

♠ K Q J 10 7 4
♡ 9 4
◊ Q 8 7 4
♣ 8

Bid 3♠, just as you would have done over partner's 3♣ rebid. This is not forcing – you would have to cuebid 3♡ to force.

(E)	WEST	NORTH	EAST	SOUTH
		1♡	Pass	2♡
	2♠	2NT	Pass	?

♠ J 7 4
♡ Q 10 6
◊ A 9 4
♣ K 8 5 2

Bid 3 NT. Good-Bad doesn't apply after a suit is bid and raised.

(F)	WEST	NORTH	EAST	SOUTH
				1♡
	1♠	Dbl	Oass	2♡
	Dbl	2 NT	Pass	?

♠ A 6 3
♡ K Q 10 7 4 3
◊ 8 6
♣ A 5

Bid 3♣. Remember that Good-Bad is on over any action by RHO, including doubles (except penalty doubles) and redoubles. West's double on this auction is regarded as takeout. Partner might have:

♠ K 5
♡ –
◊ J 7 4 3 2
♣ Q J 10 8 4 3

(G)	WEST	NORTH	EAST	SOUTH
		1♠	2♡	Dbl
	Redbl	2 NT	Pass	?

♠ 6 2
♡ A 5
◊ K J 10 9 7 4
♣ J 4 2

Bid 3 ◇. 2 NT is Good-Bad, but you intended all along to convert clubs to diamonds.

(H)	WEST	NORTH	EAST	SOUTH
		1 ♡	1 ♠	Pass
	2 ♣	2 NT	Pass	?

♠ J 7 4 3 2
♡ J 5 3
◇ 8 4
♣ J 6 3

Bid 3 ♡. Regardless of what partner has in mind, you want to play in hearts.

We'll conclude by responding after partner bids at the three level instead of using Good-Bad 2 NT.

(A)	WEST	NORTH	EAST	SOUTH
		1 ◇	1 ♡	1 ♠
	2 ♡	3 ◇	Pass	?

♠ A 8 7 4 3
♡ K 5
◇ Q 3
♣ J 6 4 2

Bid 3 NT, secure that partner has a good hand. Standard players would have to guess here.

(B)	WEST	NORTH	EAST	SOUTH
		1 ♡	1 ♠	Dbl
	2 ♠	3 ♣	Pass	?

♠ 8 5 3
♡ Q J
◇ 10 9 7 3
♣ K Q 6 4

Bid 4 ♡ ! This feels right, once you know that partner was not merely competing. Game would be cold opposite as little as:

♠ 10 7
♡ A K 9 6 3
◇ Q
♣ A J 10 5 4

(C)	WEST	NORTH	EAST	SOUTH
				1 ♡
	1 ♠	1 NT	Pass	2 ♡
	2 ♠	3 ♡	Pass	?

♠ 8
♡ A Q J 10 7 4
◇ 9 3
♣ K Q 10 6

Bid 4♡. You weren't thinking about game earlier, but it must be worth a try after North's *encouraging* raise to 3♡.

(D)	WEST	NORTH	EAST	SOUTH
			1♠	Dbl
	2♠	3♡	3♠	?

♠ 8 4
♡ A Q 6
◇ A 10 6 4
♣ A 10 5 2

Double. Since partner should have sound values, you can afford to compete. Double must be the most flexible action, with your 3½ Quick Tricks, minimum heart length and maximum number of spades, partner should know whether to sit.

Incidentally, Good-Bad 2 NT should be Alerted just like Lebensohl. Also, one should Alert the negative inferences arising from the failure to use Good-Bad. After:

WEST	NORTH	EAST	SOUTH
	1♡	1♠	1 NT
2♠	3♣		

South should Alert and, if asked, tell the opponents that North had two ways to bid 3♣ – the way he chose suggests a better hand.

Hopefully, at this point the reader can understand the concepts and mechanics of Good-Bad 2 NT. For these brave souls who are ready to find out even more, this question and answer format may prove enlightening.

Question: Can Good-Bad 2 NT also be used when the auction is at the 1-level?

Answer: Sure, after 1 ◇ – Pass – 1 ♡ – 1 ♠ wouldn't it be nice to distinguish

♠ 6   ♡ 8 2   ◇ K Q J 10 7 4 2   ♣ A Q 5?

From

♠ 8 4   ♡ K 7   ◇ A K J 10 7 4   ♣ A Q 5?

Although with each I feel like jumping to the three level. We would like to bid a preemptive, competitive 3 ◇ with the first hand, while bidding a strong 3 ◇ with the hand with more high cards. Since the purpose of preemptive jumps is to allow the opponents as little bidding room as possible, we chose to use "inverted Good-Bad" when jumping from the one-level. Therefore, rebid 3 ◇ with the "weak" hand, while bidding a "good" 2 NT this time with the better hand.

Here are some other examples of "inverted Good-Bad" in action:

1♡ – Pass – 1 ♠ – Dbl   Bid 3♡ with

♠ 8   ♡ Q 10 9 7 5 3 2   ◇ A K J 10   ♣ 8

Bid 2 NT with

♠ A 7   ♡ A Q J 10 7 4   ◇ A J 7   ♣ 6 2

1♣ – Pass – Pass – 1 ♡   Bid 3♣ with

♠ A 7   ♡ 9 4   ◇ 10 5   ♣ A Q J 9 7 4 2

Bid 2 NT with

♠ A 8   ♡ A 7 3   ◇ 8   ♣ A K J 10 7 4 2

Question: Although "Inverted Good-Bad" does seem sensible, particularly for those of us who like to preempt, doesn't that mean that we lose the jump to 2 NT to show a balanced 18–19. How in the world do we cope with that?

Answer: It is more of a problem in theory than in practise, it just doesn't seem to occur too often. After 1♣–Pass–1♡–1♠, I would bid 3 NT with

♠ A Q 8 　　♡ A 7 　　◇ K 5 3 　　♣ A Q 10 7 4,

2◇ with

♠ A 7 4 　　♡ A 6 　　◇ A 7 4 2 　　♣ K Q J 10,

and support double holding

♠ A 6 　　♡ K 8 2 　　◇ K J 5 　　♣ A K 8 6 4.

In other words, you can usually find a reasonable alternative. If my hand was

♠ A J 9 2 　　♡ A 7 　　◇ J 6 4 　　♣ A K J 8

I would be unhappy that I couldn't bid a natural 2 NT or a penalty double. So you must choose between a leap to 3 NT or a trap pass. That may seem very extreme, but in practise someone usually finds a bid over one spade. Your partner will try hard to balance with his spade shortness.

Question: There must be other times where you would like to bid a natural 2 NT, but can't because of Good-Bad. Can you give us any helpful hints?

Answer: This certainly does happen, but if you learn to make the best of your system as opposed to fighting it, you will do just fine. After all, you probably weren't too happy when you picked up

♠ K J 9 　　♡ J 7 3 　　◇ 9 5 4 2 　　♣ K 9 7

after 2♠–Dbl–Pass–? but couldn't bid a natural, non-forcing 2 NT since you were playing Lebensohl. So instead of 2 NT, bid 3◇ after

| | 1♡ | Dbl | 2♡ | ? |

with

♠ 9 4 　　♡ A Q 6 　　◇ K J 10 8 　　♣ 8 5 4 3

and 3♣ after

| 1♣ | Pass | 1♡ | 1♠ |
| Pass | 2♣ | ? | |

with

♠ A Q 　　♡ 10 8 7 6 4 　　◇ Q 5 　　♣ K 6 5 4

Life will go on. Remember These direct three level auctions are invitational just like a natural 2 NT.

Question: Does anything special happen when the action we choose over their two level interference is a jump?

Answer: As you would expect, we simply gain a method to provide us with twice as many ways to bid each auction. After

| 1♠ | Pass | 1 NT | 2♣ |
| ? | | | |

bid 3♡ (forcing) with a rock like

♠ A K 8 5 4   ♡ A Q J 9 3   ◇ A 7   ♣ 8.

but holding

♠ K Q 10 8 7 4 3   ♡ 9   ◇ A K 9   ♣ 6 4

you can also "jump" by bidding 2 NT then 3♠.

That way you won't miss a game when all partner has is

♠ 9   ♡ K J 6   ◇ K J 6 4 3   ♣ 10 7 4 2.

Also, after 1♠–Pass–1 NT–2♣, bid a normal 3♠ with

♠ A Q J 10 7 4   ♡ A Q 9   ◇ A 6   ♣ 7 4,

After an Invitational 2 NT

One subject that always bothered me, even in my best partnerships, was deciding which bids were forcing and which were not after someone invited with 2 NT. Oh, I knew what bids meant after:

1♣	1♡
2 NT.	

We always had discussed whether we played "new minor forcing" or check-back Stayman, and anyway, *any* further action by responder was forcing in this sequence.

There were even a few other auctions that weren't too tough. After:

1♡	1♠
2♣	2 NT
3♣	

3♣ had to be non-forcing, since it would be foolish if a weak 5–5 hand had no way to escape from notrump without fear of the bidding going on forever. Of course, that meant we had to raise 2 NT to 3 NT with:

♠ A 7   ♡ A Q 9 6 4   ◇ 8   ♣ A J 7 5 2

In the auction:

1♠	1 NT (forcing)
2♣	2 NT
3♠,	

3♠ was forcing since most players understood that this showed a good 6-4. With a weak 6-4 you had to be practical and rebid spades over 1 NT.

However, after:

1♠	1 NT
2 NT	3♡

would you be confident that your partner was on the same wave length as to whether 3♡ was forcing? What about:

2♡	2♠	Pass	2 NT
Pass	3♣		

Is 3♣ forcing or not?

Theorists could debate the relative merits of the forcing vs. non-forcing treatment in both these auctions, but which treatment is best really is not the crucial factor. The key to a good partnership is not having good conventions and/or treatments – it is having a thorough understanding of the methods your pair *has* chosen to play.

With this in mind, I devised a set of rules to handle the problem. I wanted my rules to do an efficient job, of course, but practicality was relevant also. No purpose would be served if the rules were so complicated that nobody could remember them.

First I had to establish some criteria under which my rules could be applied. Here is what I came up with:

1. 2 NT had to be natural and non-forcing, though invitational.
2. 2 NT couldn't have been our side's first bid in the auction.
3. Opener's jump rebid of 2 NT, after:

1 suit	1 suit
2 NT	

would be covered by a separate set of rules. (This would be true whether or not the opponents were in the auction.)

4. Our side could not have bid and raised a suit, but preference auctions *would* apply, e.g.

1♠	1 NT
2♣	2♠
2 NT	

5. *2 NT invitational* rules would apply regardless of whether 2 NT was a jump or non-jump (but keeping in mind the exceptions above).

Here is a little additional information that should prove helpful in our study of the subject.

1. All bids that are defined as forcing after an invitational 2 NT are one-round forces only. They don't guarantee a rebid, and we can stop below game (although game will usually be reached).
2. All reverses after 2 NT are forcing.
3. N.F. stands for "not forcing."

The actual rules after *2 NT invitational* will be presented in two parts. First I'll cover the situations where the opponents have bid, which turn out to be quite straightforward. The opponents must have bid (not doubled), so that a cuebid is available to your side. They may have opened with a one-bid or a two-bid, overcalled or jump overcalled. Conventional two-suited bids of any kind by the opponents are included.

1. Any suit previously named by our side is N.F.
2. A bid in an unbid major is forcing.
3. A bid in an unbid minor is N.F.

4. A bid in an opponent's suit is a forcing cuebid, suggesting a good unbalanced hand with shortness in their suit. The hand will sometimes contain a long unbid minor.

Quiz on 2 NT invitational
When the Opponents Have Bid

For each of the following auctions, decide if it meets our criteria and the rules for forcing and non-forcing continuations apply. If they do, decide whether the last bid is forcing or non-forcing.

1.	1♣	Pass	1♦	1♥
	1♠	Pass	2 NT	Pass
	3♦?			
2.	2♥	2♠	Pass	2 NT
	Pass	3♣?		
3.	1♥	1♠	Pass	2♣
	Pass	2 NT	Pass	3♦?
4.	1♠	Dbl	Pass	2 NT
	Pass	3♦?		
5.	1♦	1♥	2 NT	Pass
	3♣?			
6.	1♠	Dbl	Pass	2 NT
	Pass	3♥?		
7.	1♥	1♠	Pass	2 NT
	Pass	3♣?		
8.	1♣	1♦	Pass	2 NT
	Pass	3♥?		
9.	1♦	1♥	1♠	Pass
	2 NT	Pass	3♣?	
10.	1♦	1♠	2♥	Pass
	2 NT	Pass	3♦?	
11.	1♣	2♣	2 NT	Pass
	3♦?			
12.	1♥	2♣	Pass	2 NT
	Pass	3♦?		
13.	1♥	2♦	Pass	2 NT
	Pass	3♣?		
14.	1♥	2♠	2 NT	Pass
	3♣?			
15.	1♦	1♥	Pass	1♠
	Pass	2 NT	Pass	3♣?

126

16.	2♡	2♠	Pass	2 NT
	Pass	3♠?		
17.	1◊	1♡	Pass	2 NT
	Pass	3◊?		
18.	1♠	2♡	Pass	2 NT
	Pass	3◊?		
19.	2♡	2 NT	Pass	3♣?
20.	1◊	1♡	Pass	2♡
	Pass	2 NT	Pass	3◊?

Answers to Invitational 2 NT Quiz

1. If 2 NT is forcing, reject. If 2 NT is not forcing, neither is 3◊, because it's an old suit.
2. N.F., clubs is an unbid minor.
3. Forcing, reverse.
4. N.F., unbid minor.
5. If 2 NT is forcing, reject. If 2 NT is not forcing, N.F. (unbid minor).
6. Forcing, unbid major.
7. N.F., unbid minor.
8. Forcing, reverse.
9. Reject, opener's jump to 2 NT.
10. N.F., old suit.
11. Forcing, reverse.
12. Forcing, reverse.
13. N.F., unbid minor.
14. N.F., unbid minor.
15. N.F., old suit.
16. N.F., old suit.
17. Forcing, cuebid.
18. N.F., unbid minor.
19. Reject, 2 NT was our side's first bid.
20. Reject, suit bid and raised.

We're now ready to study auctions which include an invitational 2 NT *where the opponents have never bid*. Remember that the same general criteria presented previously still apply. (By the way, auctions which begin with 1 NT are not governed by these rules – they already should be defined in the partnership, and they are influenced by artificial bids such as Stayman and Jacoby transfers.)

I have divided all bids which follow an invitational 2 NT into three categories:

1. New suits.
2. Bids in partner's suit.
3. Rebids of a previously-bid suit or suits.

If you have trouble understanding and/or remembering the following rules, there are examples and answers which should help to clarify them.

II. Bids after an invitational 2 NT (non-competitive auctions):

    A. New suits are *forcing*, except:
        1. When our first bid was a 1 NT response, or
        2. When we have already bid another suit twice (unless, of course, the new suit is a reverse).

    B. A return to partner's suit is *forcing* if *we* opened the bidding, *non-forcing* if *partner* opened.

    C. A rebid in a previously-bid suit is *forcing* if the suit is a *major* in which we opened the bidding and we bid another suit along the way.

A rebid in a previously-bid suit is *non-forcing* if:
1. We rebid our *second* suit (except as a reverse);
2. We bid a suit for the third time;
3. We rebid our first suit, which was a *minor*.

In order to help bewildered readers, here is a summary of the above rules, which may show the reasoning used to formulate them.

1. New suits are almost always forcing, except when we were too weak to introduce them earlier.

2. A bid in partner's suit is forcing, except when we are returning to opener's suit or to one of his suits which we may not have been "strong enough" to raise earlier.

3. "Old" suits are usually non-forcing, the only exception being when we were too strong merely to rebid our original major. Therefore, we might have chosen the less discouraging rebid in a new suit, planning to follow with a forcing rebid in our primary suit if we got a chance.

Now try these examples. First, decide whether the example auction meets our criteria and our rules may be applied. Then decide if the last bid in the auction is forcing or not and provide a reason for your answer.

Quiz on non-competitive auctions after 2 NT invitational:

1.	1 NT	2♣		2.	1♣	1♠
	2♡	2 NT			2♡	2♠
	3♡				2 NT	3♢

3.	1♡	1♠		4.	1♢	1 NT
	2♣	2♠			2♡	2 NT
	2 NT	3♡			3♢	

5.	1♠	1 NT		6.	1♢	1♠
	2 NT	3♠			2♡	2 NT
					3♢	

7.	1♡	1♠		8.	1♡	1♠
	2♡	2 NT			2♣	2♠
	3♡				2 NT	3♣

9.	1 NT	2 ◇		10.	1 ♣	1 ♠
	2 ♡	2 NT			2 ♡	2 ♠
	3 ♣				2 NT	3 ♣

11.	1 ♠	1 NT		12.	1 ♡	1 NT
	2 ♡	2 ♠			2 ♠	2 NT
	2 NT	3 ♣			3 ♣	

13.	1 ◇	1 ♡		14.	1 ♣	1 ♠
	2 ♣	2 NT			2 ♡	2 ♠
	3 ◇				2 NT	3 ♡

15.	1 ◇	1 ♡		16.	1 ♡	1 NT
	1 ♠	2 NT			2 ♠	2 NT
	3 ♣				3 ♡	

17.	1 ♣	1 ◇		18.	1 ♠	1 NT
	1 ♠	2 NT (1)			2 ♠	2 NT
	3 ◇				3 ♡	

19.	1 ◇	1 ♠		20.	1 ♣	1 NT
	2 ◇	2 NT			2 NT	3 ♣
	3 ♡					

21.	1 ◇	2 ◇		22.	1 ◇	1 ♠
	2 NT	3 ♣			2 ♣	2 NT
					3 ♠	

23.	1 ◇	1 ♡		24.	1 ◇	1 ♡
	2 ◇	2 NT			1 ♠	2 NT (1)
	3 ♡				3 ◇	

25.	1 ◇	2 NT (1)		26.	1 ◇	1 ♠
	3 ♣				2 ♣	2 NT
					3 ♡	

27.	1 ♡	1 NT		28.	1 ♡	1 NT
	2 ♣	2 NT			2 ♣	2 NT
	3 ♠				3 ◇	

| 29. | 1 ♡ | 1 NT | | 30. | 1 ♠ | 1 NT |
| | 2 NT | 3 ♣ | | | 2 NT | 3 ♡ |

(1) Non-forcing

Solutions

1. Reject, the opening bid was 1 NT.

2. N.F., another suit was previously bid twice.

3. N.F., return to opener's suit.

4. N.F., our old minor.

5. N.F., return to opener's suit (presumably based on playing constructive raises).

6. N.F., our old minor.

7. N.F., thrice-bid suit. It's easy for opener to bid 3 NT or 4 ♡ with a better hand.

8. N.F., return to opener's suit.

9. Reject, the opening bid was 1 NT.

10. N.F., opener's suit.

11. N.F., opener's suit (see #5).

12. Forcing, new suit.

13. N.F., our old minor.

14. N.F., opener's suit.

15. Forcing, reverse.

16. Forcing, rebidding a major, with another suit bid along the way (rule IIC).

17. Forcing, supporting responder's suit.

18. N.F., another suit already rebid.

19. Forcing, reverse.

20. N.F., return to opener's suit.

21. Reject, suit bid and raised.

22. Forcing, opener is supporting responder's suit.

23. Forcing, opener is supporting responder's suit.

24. N.F., our old minor.

25. Forcing, new suit.

26. Forcing, reverse (also new suit). Perhaps 0-4-5-4, 14-15 HCP.

27. Forcing, reverse (also new suit). Playing 1 NT forcing without Flannery, a 4-5-1-3 14-count is quite possible.

28. Forcing, new suit.

29. N.F., first bid was a 1 NT response (rule IIA1).

30. N.F., see #29.

The Scrambling 2 NT

The next convention in our study of artificial uses for a bid of 2 NT is very straightforward, but it has proven quite helpful. It's based on the sound principle that after the opponents have bid and raised a suit and we wish to compete and/or balance, 2 NT is unlikely to be our best contract.

Therefore, we can employ 2 NT as a takeout or scrambling bid when the opponents have bid and raised a major suit. Why only a *major* suit? If the opponents have bid and raised a *minor*, we can bid our suits at the two level (unless they bid diamonds and we have clubs). It would make no sense to push unnecessarily to the three level. But after two of a major, unless we can bid 2♠ (which we'll be happy to do if possible) we must go to the three level anyway.

In order to provide an easy starting point, our initial discussion will be confined to scrambling with 2 NT over doubles.

After the opponents have raised a major to the two level and partner has doubled (takeout, penalty, responsive, negative, balancing, cooperative, etc.), a bid of 2 NT is artificial and forcing, the beginning of a scramble to locate the best available trump suit.

Here are some auctions where South might need to scramble with 2 NT.

	WEST	NORTH	EAST	SOUTH
a.	1♠	Dbl	2♠	Pass
	Pass	Dbl	Pass	?
b.			1♢	Pass
	1♠	Pass	2♠	Pass
	Pass	Dbl	Pass	?
c.	1♡	Pass	2♡	Pass
	Pass	Dbl	Pass	?
d.			1♠	Dbl
	2♠	Dbl (1)	Pass	?
e.			1♠	2♣
	2♠	Dbl (1)	Pass	?
f.				1♣
	1♡	Dbl	2♡	Pass
	Pass	Dbl (1)	Pass	?
g.	1♠	Pass	2♠	Pass
	Pass	Dbl	Redbl	?
h.			1♡	Pass
	2♡	Dbl	Pass	?
i.	1♠	2♣	2♠	Pass
	Pass	Dbl	Pass	?

(1) Responsive.

What hand would call for scrambling via 2 NT? Any hand on which South doesn't know where to play. South might have three possible trump suits, a two-suiter of some kind or even a hand with no suit at all!

Here are some examples of hands on which I would scramble by bidding 2 NT. They will correspond to the nine auctions listed above.

a.	♠ 8 6 4 2	♠ Q 7 4 2
	♡ 8	♡ J 7 3
	♢ Q 9 5 3	♢ Q 7 4
	♣ J 8 7 2	♣ 10 8 5
b.	♠ 9 7 4 3 2	♠ J 8 5
	♡ 10 7 4	♡ Q 9 3
	♢ A 6	♢ 9 4 3 2
	♣ 9 6 3	♣ Q 7 2

c.	♠ Q 4		♠ J 7
	♡ 8 6 4 3 2		♡ A Q 5
	◊ A 6 3		◊ Q 6 4 2
	♣ A 7 4		♣ J 8 7 5
d.	♠ 8		♠ A 7
	♡ A Q 8 5		♡ A K 5
	◊ A 7 4 2		◊ J 10 7 4
	♣ Q 9 6 5		♣ Q 8 4 3
e.	♠ A 5		♠ 8 5 4 3
	♡ 9 6 4		♡ 9 2
	◊ 10 5 2		◊ A 7
	♣ A K Q J 7		♣ K Q J 10 5
f.	♠ 9 4		♠ K 5
	♡ A 7		♡ 9 4 3
	◊ Q 8 5 4		◊ A K Q
	♣ A Q 8 7 2		♣ 9 7 4 3 2
g.	♠ A 7 4 2		♠ Q 7 4
	♡ 9 4 3 2		♡ A 6
	◊ 10 7 5 3		◊ Q 9 4 3
	♣ A		♣ K 5 4 2
h.	♠ A 6		♠ A 7 3
	♡ 9 4 3		♡ 6 4
	◊ J 7 5 3		◊ 10 9 8 4
	♣ 9 6 5 3		♣ 8 7 4 3
i.	♠ 8 7 3		♠ 8 6 4 2
	♡ 10 6 5 4		♡ 8 7 4
	◊ A 7 4 3		◊ K 9 6 4
	♣ J 5		♣ A 7

Are there any situations where we actually bid our suit at the three level? Of course. We do that when we're confident of which suit we want to play in. We may have a good hand or a bad hand, a good suit or a poor one, but we are in no doubt as to where to play.

Here are some examples of hands that can just bid their longest suit after:

WEST	NORTH	EAST	SOUTH
1♣	Pass	2♣	Pass
Pass	Dbl	Pass	?

♠ 8 6 4 2	♠ 10 6 2	♠ A 6 4 2
♡ 8 7 5	♡ K 9	♡ K 9 6 4 2
◊ Q 6	◊ A 7 4 3 2	◊ Q 10
♣ A K J 9	♣ K 6 3	♣ 6 3
3♣.	3◊.	3♡.

These voluntary three-level responses are often based on a five-card suit, but even a strong four-card suit isn't guaranteed – on the auction above, unless South wanted to gamble a pass, he would have to bid 3♣ on:

$\spadesuit$ 8 7 5 3 2 $\quad \heartsuit$ A 7 $\quad \diamondsuit$ A 8 $\quad \clubsuit$ J 5 4 3.

Isn't the Scrambling 2 NT really just a form of the Unusual Notrump? Sure, but there are significant differences. An Unusual Notrump bidder is acting voluntarily based on his two-suited hand. A Scrambling 2 NT bidder was forced to act by his partner and hardly can be counted on to have a two-suiter.

Conventions that enable us to avoid bad guesses as to which suit should be trumps began long ago with takeout doubles. Then came negative and responsive doubles and the Unusual Notrump. The Scrambling 2 NT merely attempts to carry on the tradition for those who don't guess so well.

Responding to a Scrambling 2 NT

If the opponents' suit is hearts, life is quite simple – the 2 NT scrambler is offering a choice of the minor suits, and must have tolerance (almost always equal length) for both. All the other hand needs to do is choose the longer minor. Therefore, after:

WEST	NORTH	EAST	SOUTH
			1 $\heartsuit$
Pass	2 $\heartsuit$	Pass	Pass
Dbl	Pass	2 NT	Pass
?			

bid 3 $\clubsuit$ with:

$\spadesuit$ J 6 4 3 $\quad \heartsuit$ 8 2 $\quad \diamondsuit$ K 7 5 $\quad \clubsuit$ A Q 9 4

and 3 $\diamondsuit$ with:

$\spadesuit$ A J 7 $\quad \heartsuit$ 9 $\quad \diamondsuit$ J 7 4 3 2 $\quad \clubsuit$ K 6 4 2.

Also bid 3 $\diamondsuit$ with:

$\spadesuit$ J 7 4 3 $\quad \heartsuit$ A $\quad \diamondsuit$ Q J 10 9 $\quad \clubsuit$ J 6 4 3.

We might as well try to play in our strongest trump suit – this is definitely not an *up-the-line* situation.

However, up-the-line does become a factor when the opponents' suit is spades. Now the scrambler may be three-suited, two-suited or have no suit at all. Therefore, the usual policy should be to respond in the cheapest suit of four or more cards. After:

WEST	NORTH	EAST	SOUTH
			1 $\spadesuit$
Pass	2 $\spadesuit$	Pass	Pass
Dbl	Pass	2 NT	Pass
?			

bid 3 $\clubsuit$ with:

$\spadesuit$ 6 $\quad \heartsuit$ A Q 9 2 $\quad \diamondsuit$ 10 8 6 5 $\quad \clubsuit$ Q J 8 3

and with:

$\spadesuit$ 8 $\quad \heartsuit$ A Q 10 $\quad \diamondsuit$ 9 7 6 4 3 $\quad \clubsuit$ K 8 5 4.

It is tempting to bid 3 ◊ with the second hand, but partner could have:

♠ A 7 4 3   ♡ 8 6 4 3   ◊ A   ♣ 10 7 6 2.

When the scrambler is two-suited (other than with spades) any combination of suits is possible.

Here are some scrambling auctions which show both the doubler and the scrambler in action.

WEST	NORTH	EAST	SOUTH
			1♠
Dbl	2♠	Pass	Pass
Dbl	Pass	2 NT	Pass
3 ◊			

♠ 9	♠ 7 6 3 2
♡ A J 6 2	♡ 8 5 4
◊ A 8 6 5 4	◊ 9 7 2
♣ A K 3	♣ Q J 10

Without the 2 NT Scramble, East would be in an impossible situation after the second double and would presumably bid clubs, his strongest and cheapest "suit." West would have no reason to disturb this.

WEST	NORTH	EAST	SOUTH
			1♠
Pass	2♠	Pass	Pass
Dbl	Pass	2 NT	Pass
3♣	Pass	3 ◊	Pass
3 ♡			

♠ 8 7	♠ 9 5 3
♡ A J 10 5	♡ 8 6 4 3
◊ K 9 4	◊ A Q 6 3
♣ Q 6 4 3	♣ A 10

East's auction suggests the red suits, and West is happy to choose hearts. Many players simply would bid 3 ♡ with the East cards after the balancing double, assuming that West had four hearts, but there are many hands where West should balance with a double though holding only three hearts. Following are two examples.

WEST	NORTH	EAST	SOUTH
			1♠
Pass	2♠	Pass	Pass
Dbl	Pass	2 NT	Pass
3 ◊			

♠ 7 5 4	♠ 9 2
♡ A 10 8	♡ J 6 4
◊ K 10 9 3	◊ A 7 4 2
♣ K 7 2	♣ A Q 6 5

WEST	NORTH	EAST	SOUTH
			1♠
Pass	2♣	Pass	Pass
Dbl	Pass	2 NT	Pass
3◇			

♠ 8 5 4	♠ 9
♡ A K J	♡ 10 7 4 3
◇ Q J 10 2	◇ A 7 4 3
♣ Q 10 9	♣ K 8 5 4

The second auction above shows how efficiently the Scrambling 2 NT handles the three-suiters as well.

Our new device also comes in handy when running from partner's penalty double. Wouldn't you like to have a takeout available in the following situations?

WEST	NORTH	EAST	SOUTH
	1♠	Pass	Pass
2♡	2♠	Dbl	Pass
?			

♠ –	♡ A K Q J 6	◇ 9 7 4 3	♣ 8 5 4 2

WEST	NORTH	EAST	SOUTH
		1◇	Pass
1♡	2♠	Dbl	Pass
?			

♠ 3	♡ J 9 6 4 3	◇ J 6 4	♣ Q J 10 6

Of course, it could be right to pass partner's double in either of these cases, but letting the opponents play at the two level, doubled, when they probably have at last eight trumps may not be the best way to keep partners and/or teammates.

I promised to mention some auctions where the Scrambling 2 NT may be employed after partner has done something other than double. In the examples below, the 2 NT bids may be treated as Scrambling.

WEST	NORTH	EAST	SOUTH
Pass	Pass	2♡	Pass
Pass	2♠	Pass	Pass
2 NT			

♠ 8	♡ 6 3	◇ A J 10 6 4	♣ K J 10 7 5

2 NT would show the minors, presumably with heart tolerance.

WEST	NORTH	EAST	SOUTH
	1♡	Pass	2♡
Pass	Pass	2♠	Pass
2 NT			

♠ Q	♡ 7 3	◇ A 9 7 5 4	♣ K 8 7 4 3

Spades is unlikely to be the right spot when partner failed to overcall 1♠. 2 NT asks partner to pick a minor suit.

WEST	NORTH	EAST	SOUTH
			1♣
Pass	2♦	Pass	Pass
2 NT			

♠ 8 7 4   ♡ K Q J 6   ◇ 9   ♣ A J 7 4 3

In the balancing seat, 2 NT shows a two-suiter but not necessarily the minors. A balancing double could lead to disaster opposite a hand like:

♠ K 5   ♡ 7 4   ◇ Q 8 7 4 3 2   ♣ K 10 6

WEST	NORTH	EAST	SOUTH
		1NT	Pass
2◇ (1)	Pass	2♡	Pass
Pass	2♠	Pass	2NT

(1) transfer

♠ 8   ♡ J 9 7   ◇ A J 10 6   ♣ 8 5 4 3 2

A Scrambling 2 NT seems more flexible than 3♣. 2 NT is not needed as a natural bid here, since with a decent balanced hand we can try a cooperative double.

WEST	NORTH	EAST	SOUTH
		1◇	1♠
Dbl (1)	2♠	Pass	Pass
2 NT			

(1) negative

♠ 8   ♡ A Q 7 4   ◇ K 10 3   ♣ 9 8 6 5 4

It can't be right to sell out to 2♠, and we'd need another spade for a second double (in case partner elects to pass for penalties). Why guess between 3♣ and 3◇?

Though our last 2 NT example could be classed as a Scramble, it already is well-defined in the expert community as a type of Unusual Notrump. After:

WEST	NORTH	EAST	SOUTH
			1♠
2♣	2♠	Pass	Pass
?			

bid 2 NT with:

♠ 9		♠ 9
♡ A K J 6	or	♡ 8 5
◇ 8 5		◇ A K J 6
♣ A Q 8 7 4 2		♣ A Q 8 7 4 2

Partner can bid past 3♣ only if he is prepared for either red suit.

To sum up, the Scrambling 2 NT requires very little memory work and can prove helpful in avoiding nasty guesses in the selection of a trump suit. All that is lost is the use of 2 NT as a natural bid, a small price to pay. It's just one more example of how 2 NT can be used as an artificial aid to better bidding.

The Jacoby 2 NT Response Revisited

As a longtime advocate of bids showing fit, I've always like the concept of the Jacoby 2 NT response as a forcing raise of opener's major. Responder promises at least an opening bid with four-card support or better and suggests balanced or semibalanced pattern (especially if *splinter* responses are also available). Opener can show a singleton (or void) or a side five-card suit with his rebid. With balanced (5-3-3-2) and semibalanced (usually 5-4-2-2 or 6-3-2-2) patterns, he tries to show his approximate high-card strength.

Here's how it works after:

OPENER	RESPONDER
1♠	2 NT

3♣, 3♢, 3♡	=	shortness in the bid suit.
4♣, 4♢, 4♡	=	second five-card suit.
3♠, 3 NT, 4♠	=	balanced or semibalanced patterns, 3♠ is the strongest rebid, 4♠ is the weakest.

Unfortunately, my experience suggests that this widely-played rebidding schedule may not work so well. Here are some problems I've encountered.

(A) When opener shows an unbalanced hand, he says nothing about his high-card strength. He must rebid 3♢ with both:

♠ A K J 7 4   ♡ K 9 5 3   ♢ 8   ♣ 10 7 4

and

♠ A K J 7 4   ♡ K J 8 6   ♢ 8   ♣ A 8 5;

or 4♢ with both:

♠ J 8 6 4 3   ♡ 8   ♢ A K Q 7 4   ♣ Q 5

and

♠ A K 10 7 3   ♡ 8   ♢ A K J 6 5   ♣ 6 3.

(B) There is no way for opener to show an extra (sixth) trump, which may be crucial for slam purposes.

(C) Responder can never say anything about his distribution, when often it is *his* ruffing values which determine slam chances.

(D) Space-consuming jumps to the four level are too frequent. Not only does the jump showing a second suit severely crowd the bidding, but slam exploration is very difficult after opener's jump to four of his major. I often hold promising hands like:

♠ A K 7 4 3   ♡ K Q J 6 5   ◊ 8 3   ♣ 9,

and have to worry about being cold for seven opposite a respectable hand like:

♠ J 10 8 6 5   ♡ A 8   ◊ A 6 4   ♣ A 8 5,

but having no play at the five level opposite a dog like:

♠ Q J 9 5 2   ♡ A 7 4   ◊ Q 7   ♣ K J 6.

After consideration of the problem at length, consultation with friends who offered alternatives, and several revisions, I emerged with a "New Jacoby 2 NT" structure. Actually, the finished product bears little resemblance to the familiar Jacoby 2 NT rebid structure outlined above. However, I am confident that my suggested structure represents a significant improvement.

To enable the reader to understand the overall structure, here is a list of hand types for opener that I set out to identify and distinguish among:

(a) two-suiters, more than minimum strength
(b) hands with singletons, more than minimum strength
(c) hands with singletons, minimum strength
(d) hands with voids
(e) goodish hands with a six-card suit
(f) balanced or semibalanced hands with great strength. (If 5–3–3–2, then 17–18 HCP)
(g) minimum hands with poor controls
(h) minimum hands, but with some slam potential

Also, my structure provides opener with the opportunity to learn something about responder's distribution, as well as giving responder a chance to make asking bids, which may be valuable after he chooses to start with a Jacoby 2 NT response on a hand like:

♠ A 8 7 6 4 3   ♡ 7 4   ◊ –   ♣ A K 7 5 3

Here we go.

OPENER	RESPONDER
1♠	2 NT

Opener rebids	with:
3♣	non-minimums with singletons OR big balanced or semibalanced hands.
3◊	non-minimum two-suiters OR *any* good hand that is anxious to learn more about responder's distribution.

3 ♡	all hands with voids.
3 ♠	all minimums with singletons.
3 NT	good hands with a six-card suit.
4 ♣, 4 ♦	decent minimums, identifying cheaper ace or king.
4 ♡	decent minimums with no control in a minor suit.
4 ♠	signoff.

Of course, you need to know the way opener identifies the location of his shortness or his second suit, in addition to distinguishing the different balanced hands shown by the 3 ♣ rebid. But that will have to wait. For the time being, we will give examples of the rebids listed above in order to help clarify what they mean.

Assume in each case that you have opened 1 ♠ and your partner has responded 2 NT, Jacoby. Choose your rebid based on Jacoby Revised.

(1)   ♠ K Q 8 6 4   ♡ A J 5   ◊ 5   ♣ A 10 7 4

3 ♣. A decent hand with a singleton.

(2)   ♠ A Q 7 4 3   ♡ A 10 6   ◊ K 5   ♣ 4 3 2

4 ◊. A reasonable minimum with no club control.

(3)   ♠ A 10 6 5 3   ♡ Q J 6 4 3   ◊ −   ♣ A 10 6

3 ♡. Shows a void somewhere. Though voids seldom occur, I believe they are significant enough that it is correct to distinguish them from singletons. Temporarily, we'll lump all hands with voids together under one rebid.

(4)   ♠ A Q 10 7 4   ♡ K 7 5   ◊ 9 6   ♣ Q J 8

4 ♠. Try to turn partner off.

(5)   ♠ A K 7 4 3   ♡ A Q 6 3   ◊ 8 4   ♣ 7 3

3 ◊. 5–4 pattern qualfies as a two-suiter, and the strength is just acceptable for the non-minimum 3 ◊ rebid.

(6)   ♠ A K 7 4 3   ♡ K Q J   ◊ K J 7   ♣ 8 5

3 ♣. You will get to show the balanced nature of your good hand on the next round.

(7)   ♠ A K 7 4 2   ♡ K Q 10   ◊ Q 6   ♣ 4 3 2

4 ♡. A decent minimum with no minor-suit control.

(8)   ♠ Q J 6 5 4   ♡ A J 7 4   ◊ 6   ♣ K J 5

3 ♠. A minimum hand with a singleton.

(9)   ♠ A Q 10 6 4 3   ♡ A 7 4   ◊ K 6   ♣ J 10

3 NT. A goodish hand with a six-card suit.

(10)   ♠ Q 10 6 4 2   ♡ A 7   ◊ 8   ♣ A K 9 4 2

3 ◊. This rebid is best on most 5–5 hands.

(11)   ♠ A Q 10 5 4   ♡ 8 4   ◊ A J 6 3   ♣ Q 5

4 ◊. Not good enough for 3 ◊ but too good for 4 ♠.

(12)   ♠ A J 7 4 3 2   ♡ 9 5 3 2   ◇ A 6   ♣ A

3 ◇. This is close. You could bid 3 ♣ to show a singleton, but I'm never anxious to splinter with a singleton ace. 3 NT is also possible, to show the six-card suit. I prefer 3 ◇ because I'm eager to learn if partner has a doubleton heart.

Now it's time to examine the further development of the auction from responder's point of view.

OPENER REBIDS 3 ♣:

As you recall, this promises either a good hand with a singleton (not a void) OR a very good balanced or semibalanced hand. The hands with singletons promise 13 or more HCP (no upper limit). If the singleton is an honor, a better hand is required. The balanced hands should contain 17+ to 19 HCP, the semibalanced hands (5-4-2-2) about 15-17 HCP. Here are some examples:

1.	♠ A Q 7 4 3	2.	♠ K J 9 7 4
	♡ K Q 10		♡ A 6
	◇ 8 5		◇ A Q J 5
	♣ A Q 6		♣ J 6
3.	♠ A 10 6 4 3	4.	♠ A K J 7 4
	♡ A J		♡ A 6
	◇ K J 10		◇ J 3
	♣ K Q J		♣ K J 5 3

While these hands would be very interested in slam, they wouldn't be willing to *force* to slam.

We're now ready to see how responder rebids after opener's 3 ♣. First, he'll make an asking rebid of 3 ◇. He will do this on virtually all hands. (Later in this series we'll encounter one exception.)

After:

OPENER	RESPONDER
1 major	2 NT
3 ♣	3 ◇

3 ♡ – singleton club
3 ♠ – singleton diamond
3 NT – singleton in the other major
4 ♣ – balanced or semibalanced hand with club control
4 ◇ – balanced or semibalanced hand, diamond control, no club control
4 ♡ – balanced or semibalanced hand, no minor-suit control (rare)

Note that this is the same concept for showing shortness (via *splinter relays*) that we used after some of our other major-suit raises. A similar schedule will also be utilized after opener's 3 ♡ and 3 ♠ rebids.

140

OPENER REBIDS 3 ◊:

This is the most revolutionary idea in "Jacoby 2 NT Revised." The bid asks *responder* to describe his distribution. It can be used by opener with any good hand on which he is anxious to discover the presence or absence of specific doubletons. Typically, opener holds a two-suiter. Here are some example hands:

5. ♠ A K 7 4 3
   ♡ A K 6 4 2
   ◊ 8 5
   ♣ 9

6. ♠ K 10 6 4 3 2
   ♡ A
   ◊ K 6 5 3
   ♣ 9 4

7. ♠ A 6
   ♡ A 10 9 4 3
   ◊ A Q
   ♣ 8 6 4 3

8. ♠ 9 4
   ♡ K Q 9 5 3
   ◊ K Q 7 4
   ♣ A 7

After:

OPENER	RESPONDER
1 ♠	2 NT
3 ◊	

3 ♡ – doubleton club
3 ♠ – doubleton diamond
3 NT – doubleton heart
4 ♣ – non-minimum 4-3-3-3 (15+ HCP)
4 ◊ – singleton club, good hand
4 ♡ – singleton diamond, good hand
4 ♠ – minimum 4-3-3-3 (13-14 HCP)

If you're surprised that responder may have a singleton for his 2 NT response, it's because our splinter bids are quite limited. I would splinter in response to 1 ♠ with:

9. ♠ K 10 6 4
   ♡ A J 7 2   or
   ◊ A 8 6 3
   ♣ 9

10. ♠ A Q 7 3 2
    ♡ A 10 6
    ◊ 9 7 4 3
    ♣ 8

but

11. ♠ A 10 6 4
    ♡ A Q 3
    ◊ A 9 7 4 3
    ♣ 9

is definitely too good in our style. With the better hands, we prefer to go slower and save bidding room.

If the opening bid is 1 ♡, only a club singleton can be *shown* after 3 ◊ since we never want to go past four of the trump suit at this point.

OPENER REBIDS 3♡:

This shows a void somewhere, with any strength or distribution possible. After 3♡, responder always bids 3♠ to ask for the location of the void.

OPENER	RESPONDER
1 major	2 NT
3♡	3♠

3 NT – club void
4♣ – diamond void
4◊ – void in the other major

OPENER REBIDS 3♠:

This promises an unspecified singleton but only a minimum hand. Therefore, responder is under no obligation to try for slam. He will do so only with a very good raise on which slam can be made opposite the right shortness.

After:

OPENER	RESPONDER
1♡	2 NT
3♠	

I would sign off in 4♡ with the following:

12. ♠ K 8 5
    ♡ K Q 7 4
    ◊ A 6
    ♣ K 9 4 3

13. ♠ A Q 6 3 2
    ♡ A 10 6 3
    ◊ Q 5
    ♣ Q 6

14. ♠ K Q 6
    ♡ Q J 7 5 4
    ◊ K Q 9
    ♣ K 2

However, the following hands *would* be suitable to *relay with 3 NT* after the auction above:

15. ♠ A 6 4 3
    ♡ A K 7 4
    ◊ 9 5 4
    ♣ A 6

16. ♠ A 7 4 2
    ♡ A 9 8 4 3
    ◊ A 6
    ♣ K 5

17. ♠ K Q 5
    ♡ 10 9 8 6 2
    ◊ A J 7 4
    ♣ A

Opener shows his singleton, of course, with splinter relays, which in this case:

OPENER	RESPONDER
1 ♡	2 NT
3 ♣	3 NT

results in:

4 ♣ – singleton club
4 ◇ – singleton diamond
4 ♡ – singleton spade

OPENER REBIDS 4♣ OR HIGHER:

After one of opener's higher rebids, responder already knows a good deal about opener's hand and all his rebids are merely cuebids. As you would expect, a return to four of the trump suit is the weakest action. (One word about cuebidding style – we prefer to cuebid our cheapest ace or king, as long as the king is not opposite partner's singleton. After all, we can always use Blackwood to discover if too many aces are missing.)

Time for some well-bid hands using *Jacoby 2 NT Revised*. As you examine the following auctions, you might try to imagine how pairs using Standard Jacoby would do.

	OPENER			RESPONDER
1.	♠ A J 8 6 4 3			♠ K 10 7 5
	♡ K 6			♡ A 8 4 3
	◇ K 8 4 2			◇ A 6
	♣ A			♣ J 7 4

1 ♠	2 NT
3 ◇	3 ♠
4 NT	5 ♣
7 ♠	Pass

Opener had a choice of rebids over 2 NT. He selected 3 ◇ because he was so anxious to learn if responder had a doubleton diamond. When his prayers were duly answered (by responder's 3 ♠ bid), it was child's play to use Key Card Blackwood and reach the excellent grand slam.

2.	♠ K 8 6 3			♠ J 4
	♡ K Q 10 7 2			♡ A J 8 4
	◇ K 5 2			◇ A Q J 9
	♣ 6			♣ J 7 4

1 ♡	2 NT
3 ♠	4 ♡
Pass	

After 3 ♠, responder knew there couldn't be a slam regardless of which singleton opener had. The partnership just couldn't have enough high-card values. After a Standard Jacoby 2 NT auction (beginning with 1 ♡ –2 NT, 3 ♣), might not some pairs reach the five level with these cards?

3. ♠ A J 7 4 3 2   ♠ 10 8 6 5
    ♡ 6 4   ♡ A K 5 2
    ◇ A K 5   ◇ 4 3
    ♣ 5 3   ♣ A K 8

1 ♠	2 NT
3 NT	4 ♣
4 ◇	4 ♡
4 ♠	4 NT
5 ♡	6 ♠
Pass	

Responder's hand improved nicely after he learned that opener had a sixth trump and a respectable hand. After responder ascertained that opener had a diamond control also, he knew that slam rated to be a good contract.

4. ♠ A Q 9 7 3   ♠ K 10 8 6 5 2
    ♡ A 6 4 2   ♡ 8 3
    ◇ –   ◇ K 7 5 4
    ♣ J 8 5 4   ♣ A

1 ♠	2 NT
3 ♡	3 ♠
4 ♣	4 ◇
4 ♡	4 NT
5 ♠	5 NT
6 ♠	Pass

3♡ showed a void somewhere and 4♣ pinpointed it in diamonds. 4◇ was merely a waiting bid, since there is no point in cuebidding a control opposite partner's known void. 4♡ was the cuebid that responder wanted to hear, and after opener showed two aces, responder only needed to discover one king to bid a grand. 6♠ denied any kings (using the improved king-ask) so the partnership settled for 6♠.

5. ♠ A K 9 4 3   ♠ Q J 7 2
    ♡ A Q 5   ♡ K 3
    ◇ 10 7 4   ◇ A K Q J
    ♣ 8 5   ♣ Q 7 4

1 ♠	2 NT
4 ♡	4 ♠
Pass	

It's fun to bid and make good slams, but it's also good bridge to avoid bad ones. Responder was hopeful about slam with his monster, but when opener denied any minor-suit controls with his 4♡ rebid, responder knew to stop in 4♠.

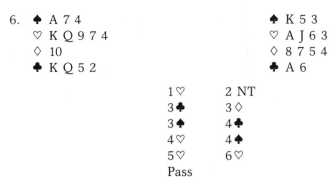

6.   ♠ A 7 4   ♠ K 5 3
     ♡ K Q 9 7 4   ♡ A J 6 3
     ◊ 10   ◊ 8 7 5 4
     ♣ K Q 5 2   ♣ A 6

1 ♡	2 NT
3 ♣	3 ◊
3 ♠	4 ♣
4 ♡	4 ♠
5 ♡	6 ♡
Pass	

Once responder knew that opener had a reasonable hand with a singleton diamond, he could afford to bid aggressively. 4 ♠ was "kickback" in hearts. (After 1 ♡ – 2 NT, all 4 ♠ bids are Roman Key Card Blackwood.)

Many Standard Jacoby 2 NT pairs would reach slam after starting with:

1 ♡ – 2 NT,   3 ◊ – 3 ♡,   3 ♠ – 4 ♣; but responder would have to worry that opener might hold a minimum like:

♠ A J 6   ♡ K Q 9 7 4   ◊ 10   ♣ Q 5 4 2,

while opener wouldn't know about the perfect fit opposite. As is quite often the case, it would be more efficient for one player to tell a great deal about his hand than for both hands to try to pass information back and forth.

7.   ♠ A Q 6 4 2   ♠ J 10 7 5
     ♡ A 8   ♡ K 10 4
     ◊ J 7   ◊ A K 9
     ♣ K Q J 5   ♣ A 7 3

1 ♠	2 NT
3 ♣	3 ◊
4 ♣	4 ◊
4 ♡	4 NT
5 ♠	6 NT
Pass	

By the time responder used Blackwood, he knew that opener had a very good balanced or semibalanced hand with at least the ♣K and ♡A. After learning that one key card was missing, it was easy for him not only to bid slam but also to try 6 NT. Being in notrump instead of a suit can be crucial with such hands at matchpoints.

8.   ♠ K J 9 6 2   ♠ A 8 7 5 4 3
     ♡ A 8 6 2   ♡ Q J
     ◊ A J 10   ◊ —
     ♣ 6   ♣ A K 7 5 3

1 ♠	2 NT
3 ♣	3 NT
4 ♣	5 ♣
5 ♠	7 ♠
Pass	

After opener's 3♣ rebid, responder is usually expected to bid 3◊, allowing opener to clarify his hand-type. Only possession of a very unusual hand, such as the one above, can explain responder's failure to do so. Therefore, any action over 3♣ other than 3◊ is an *asking bid*, based on our splinter relay principle.

After opener's 3♣ rebid:

3◊ = usual inquiry
3♡ = (step 1) asking in clubs
3♠ = (step 2) asking in diamonds
3 NT = (step 3) asking in the other major

Opener answers these asking bids as follows:

step 1 = no control
step 2 = third-round control (queen or doubleton)
step 3 = second-round control (king or singleton)
step 4 = first-round control (ace)

Asking bids also can be used when opener rebids 3♡ or 3♠ over 2 NT. After:

OPENER	RESPONDER
1 major	2 NT
3♡	?

3♠ = asking for location of void, as usual
3 NT = asking in clubs
4♣ = asking in diamonds
4◊ = asking in the other major

After:

OPENER	RESPONDER
1 major	2 NT
3♠	?

3 NT = asking for location of singleton, as usual
4♣ = asking in clubs
4◊ = asking in diamonds
4♡ = asking in hearts if spades are trumps; signoff if hearts are trumps

In example 8, therefore, 3 NT asked about hearts and 4♠ (step 4) showed the ace. 5♣ was a natural asking bid and 5♠ (step 3) promised a singleton or the king. Responder now knew that opener had a non-minimum opener with a singleton club and the ♡A. 7♠ was the indicated action, which rated to be (and was) ice-cold.

To finish this discussion of our version of the Jacoby 2 NT response, we'll look at how to cope if the opponents interfere.

A. If the opponents double 2 NT

This is the easiest interference to deal with. Opener merely can make the same bid he would have made without the double. He does have a new option, a redouble, and this should show a minimum balanced hand (5-3-3-2). We may have a chance to teach the opponents a lesson for stepping into our action, even if they have a fit.

If doubler's partner does bid, all doubles are penalty-oriented. If responder wishes to learn more about opener's hand, he can pass over doubler's partner's bid as a relay. For example:

WEST	NORTH	EAST	SOUTH
			1 ♠
Pass	2 NT	Dbl	3 ♣
3 ◊	Pass	Pass	3 ♡

Opener's 3 ♡ would show a singleton club, as if responder had relayed with 3 ◊.

B. If the opponents overcall at the three level.

For the sake of simplicity, I suggest that all of opener's actions remain the same, regardless of whether the overcall is above or below our suit, or even if the opponents cuebid our suit.

Opener's priorities:

1. *Double* . . . with a minimum balanced hand. This is opener's worst hand from an offensive point of view. Take ths action even if your doubleton is in the opponent's suit and regardless of your honor holding. Responder now should be in good position to pass the double, bid 3 NT (to play) or proceed to four of the trump suit. If responder does continue to look for slam, opener can be sure his partner has a *very* strong hand.

2. *Bid 3 NT* . . . with a singleton or void in the opponent's suit and at least a respectable opening bid. If the opponent's overcall was a cuebid of our suit, then we assume that their suit was the other major. So after:

WEST	NORTH	EAST	SOUTH
			1 ♠
Pass	2 NT	3 ♠	?

3 NT by South promises heart shortness and would be appropriate with:

> ♠ A K 7 4 3   ♡ 8   ◊ A Q 6 3   ♣ 10 7 4

3. *Bid four of our trump suit* . . . with a minimum opener and only five trumps. However, this promises shape (since all minimum 5-3-3-2 hands double). Therefore, after:

WEST	NORTH	EAST	SOUTH
			1 ♡
Pass	2 NT	3 ◊	?

I'd bid 4 ♡ with:

> ♠ K Q 10 4   ♡ A Q 10 3 2   ◊ J 5   ♣ 8 3   or

> ♠ K 9 4   ♡ A J 7 4 3   ◊ 8   ♣ Q J 7 3,   but not with

> ♠ A 6 3   ♡ A 10 9 7 4 3   ◊ K 3   ♣ 4 2,

since possession of a sixth trump is important enough to warrant a special rebid of its own . . .

4. *Rebid in the cheapest suit . . .* with a six-card trump suit. Opener still could have a minimum hand, but experience has shown that knowledge of the extra trump will help partner immensely in making both five-level and slam decisions.

5. *Rebid in a new suit, but not the cheapest one . . .* with shortness (singleton or void) in the just bid suit and a decent hand. We won't always be able to do this, but since it isn't really necessary to go out of our way to cuebid (we can always to that later), we might as well make this splinter bid when we have a chance. So after:

WEST	NORTH	EAST	SOUTH
			1 ♡
Pass	2 NT	3 ♠	?

Dbl = minimum hand, some 5-3-3-2 pattern
3 NT = spade shortness, decent hand
4 ♣ = six-card trump suit
4 ◊ = diamond shortness, decent hand
4 ♡ = minimum hand, some shape

6. *Pass . . .* with a good hand, only five trumps and no singleton or void (unless there is no room to show it). This action invites cuebidding but partner is able to double for penalty. The important principle is that we are always free to pass rather than cuebid. We can always do that later on.

C. The opponents bid at the four level below our suit.

Further agreements are needed when the opponents have jumped to the four level. If their suit is only *one* step below our trump suit (as in this auction: 1 ♡ -Pass-2 NT-4 ◊), we must be practical and revise our rebids accordingly.

Dbl = two or more cards in their suit. This suggests defending and implies a minimum hand.
4 ♡ = good offense but may be minimum.
Pass = slam interest, often shortness in their suit.

When their suit is *two* more steps below our trump suit, we're slightly more comfortable. We can still tell partner about the important sixth trump by bidding the cheapest suit.

D. The opponents bid at the four level above our suit.

We can't play in four of our suit anymore. Now we must use Forcing Pass measures.

Dbl . . . shows an offensive minimum and suggests defending.
Pass . . . suggests more offense.
A bid . . . should promise real slam interest, with a two-suiter.
Pass, then a pull of partner's double . . . is a cuebid, with lots of high cards.

The following chart summarizes the methods we have discussed. Opener's action after a double is omitted, since that involves few problems.

| OPENER'S ACTION | OPPONENT'S BID OVER JACOBY 2 NT REVISED | | | |
	Three-level Overcall	Four-level Overcall one step below	Four-level Overcall two or three steps below	Four of our suit or higher
3 NT	Shortness in their suit, good opening	–	–	–
Four of trump suit	minimum hand, not 5-3-3-2	good offense, may be minimum	minimum hand, not 5-3-3-2	–
Cheapest suit	six-card suit, could be a minimum hand	–	six-card suit, avoid with minimum hand	two-suiter
Double	5-3-3-2, minimum hand	two+ cards, bad hand for offense	two+ cards, bad hand for offense	minimum offense, suggests defending
Pass	five trumps slam interest	–	slam interest	may not be slam interest
Another suit	shortness in bid suit, decent hand	–	splinter (rare)	two-suiter

BRIDGE BOOKS AVAILABLE FROM MAX HARDY, PUBLISHER
Post Office Box 28219, Las Vegas, Nevada 89126-2219
(702) 368-0379

Bergen, Marty – **Better Bidding With Bergen** Vol I Uncontested Auctions . . . .$ 9.95
Bergen, Marty – **Better Bidding With Bergen** Vol II Competitive Bidding . . . .$ 9.95
DeSerpa, Allan – **The Mexican Contract** (novel) . . . .$ 5.95
Goldman, Bobby – **Aces Scientific** . . . .$ 9.95
Goldman, Bobby – **Winners and Losers at the Bridge Table** . . . .$ 3.95
Hardy, Max – **Two Over One Game Force, Revised and Updated** $12.95
Hardy, Max – **Forcing Notrump Responses** . . . .$ 2.95
Hardy, Max – **New Minor Forcing** . . . .$ 2.95
Hardy, Max – **Fourth Suit Forcing** . . . .$ 2.95
Hardy, Max – **Three titles above under one Cover** . . . .$ 7.95
Hardy, Max – **Splinters and Other Shortness Bids** . . . .$ 7.95
Karpin, Fred – **The Drawing of Trumps and Its Postponement** . . . .$ 9.95*
Karpin, Fred – **The Play of the Cards – Self Quizzes at Bridge** . . . .$ 9.95*
Lawrence, Mike – **The Complete Book on Balancing in Contract Bridge** . . . . . .$ 9.95
                                  (Hard Cover) $14.95
Lawrence, Mike – **The Complete Book on Overcalls in Contract Bridge** . . . .$ 9.95
                                  (Hard Cover) $14.95
Lawrence, Mike – **The Complete Book on Hand Evaluation in Contract Bridge** $ 9.95
Lawrence, Mike – **Judgement at Bridge** . . . .$ 8.95
Lawrence, Mike – **Mike Lawrence's Workbook on the Two-Over-One System** . . .$11.95
Lawrence, Mike – **Play a Swiss Teams of Four With Mike Lawrence** . . . .$ 6.95
Machlin, Jerome S. – **Tournament Bridge, an Uncensored Memoir** . . . .$ 5.95
Sontag, Alan and Steinberg, Peter – **Improve Your Bridge – Fast** . . . .$ 4.95
Stern, Milton and others – **Expert Bridge** . . . .$ 6.95
Von Elsner, Don – **The Ace of Spies** (novel) . . . .$ 5.95
Von Elsner, Don – **The Best of Jake Winkman** (anthology) . . . .$ 5.95
Von Elsner, Don – **Cruise Bridge** (novel) . . . .$ 5.95
Von Elsner, Don – **Everything's Jake With Me** (anthology) . . . .$ 5.95
Von Elsner, Don – **The Jack of Hearts** (novel) . . . .$ 5.95
Von Elsner, Don – **The Jake of Diamonds** (novel) . . . .$ 5.95

*Limited supply available at $6.95

For single copy orders include $1.50 for postage and handling. Nevada residents add 6% sales
tax. Orders of $25.00 or more deduct 10%. Orders of $50.00 or more deduct 20%.